Scottish Women

A Very Peculiar History®

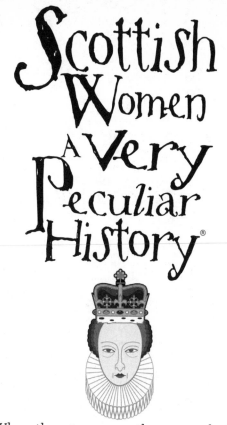

'Where there is a woman, there is mischief.'

Scotland's favourite holy man, St Colomba (c 521–597)

To all unsung Scottish heroines,
past and present.

FM

For Shirley Salariya, Ellena Salariya,
Beatrice Salariya and Gladys Stewart.

DS

Editor: Nick Pierce
Artist: David Lyttleton
Additional artwork: Shutterstock

Published in Great Britain in MMXIX by
Book House, an imprint of
The Salariya Book Company Ltd
25 Marlborough Place, Brighton BN1 1UB
www.salariya.com

ISBN: 978-1-912537-39-6

SALARIYA

SCRIBO BOOK HOUSE SCRIBBLERS

1 3 5 7 9 8 6 4 2

A CIP catalogue record for this book is available
from the British Library.

Printed and bound in China.
Printed on paper from sustainable sources.

Visit
www.salariya.com
for our online catalogue and
free fun stuff.

Scottish Women
A Very Peculiar History®

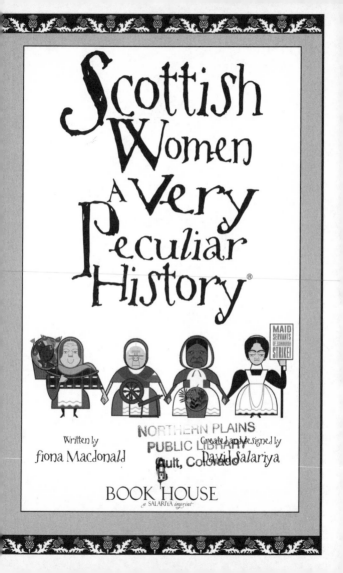

Written by
Fiona Macdonald

Created and designed by
David Salariya

BOOK HOUSE
a SALARIYA imprint

'Now of wemen this
I say for me,
Of erthly thingis
nane may bettir be. '

Scotland's most famous early (c 1500) poet,
William Dunbar

Nane = none

Contents

6 We love this piece,
but it's far too
Scottish for us. 9

*Remark allegedly made to Scottish poet
Liz Lochhead about her play featuring
the best-known Scottish woman ever,
anywhere:* Mary Queen of Scots got her
Head Chopped Off.

See page 8

'REPUTATIONS AND REMEMBERING'*

'Far too Scottish???!!!' Yes, Scots women, from queens to beggars, certainly were Scottish, but that doesn't make them a different species. They lived at particular times, in particular places, and their ideas, beliefs, words and actions were of course shaped by their surroundings. Shaped, but not limited. The doings of Scottish women have had an influence far beyond 'the great little country' that was their homeland. Just like (if we may be both sentimental and stereotypical) ripples spreading outwards from a shining Cairngorm pebble dropped into the clear and chilly waters of a Highland loch.

* *Historian Sue Innes (1948–2005) describing work on the first-ever* Biographical Dictionary of Scottish Women, *Edinburgh University Press 2006 & 2007.*

'Strange people'?

However, the criticism faced by Liz Lochhead about her play was not personal to her, or even new. For centuries, especially to the English, Scottish people have been 'the other', caricatured and misunderstood. Looking back over his early life in 1877, Scottish geologist Hugh Miller recalled a casual remark made to him by an English traveller: 'You Scotch are strange people…'. At that time, the majority of non-Scots would very probably have shared those views; do traces of them still linger?

Scots or not?

So, then. What makes a woman – or a man, or a child – Scottish rather than simply British? Traditionally, place of birth and upbringing. Until recently, being born in Scotland and being raised and educated there were assumed to guarantee a special and uniquely Scottish culture, accent, vocabulary and outlook. That once may well have been true, but now, when every aspect of our lives is shaped by international social media and digital communications, local customs, accents, standards and traditions are all rapidly blending and blurring, for good or ill.

In the past (and even now, when it comes to picking sports teams) Scottishness might also be claimed through heritage. For centuries, there have been many more people of Scottish descent living outside Scotland than within its boundaries. Today, Scots-by-ancestry outnumber people living within the boundaries of Scotland by about ten to one. Their views of Scotland, and the 'Scottish' traditions that they follow in their current homelands, may be very different from those of Scottish residents today. But does that matter? After all, the Scottish Government's own website declares:

> **Scottishness is a state of mind.**

However, in this little book, we have only limited space. So we will follow the Scottish Government and include only women of Scottish birth and upbringing, or women who may have been born elsewhere but who chose to spend most of their lives in Scotland.

Adopted Scots

In one sense, all Scots are immigrants. For 12,000 years, maybe more, settlers, conquerors, migrants and refugees have all chosen to live in Scotland. Many – we don't know precisely how many – were women.

The most famous must be **Queen Victoria** (1819–1901), born in London of German and English ancestry. She fell in love with Scotland's scenery, built a wildly romantic castle, and, by making Scotland fashionable, almost single-handedly created the Scottish tourist industry.

Hundreds of years before, women from much further afield were at the Scottish royal court. For example, in 1512, King James V gave money and silk cloth (perhaps gifts? perhaps wages?) to **Blak Elen** and a '**blak madin**', both from Africa.

Even earlier, around AD 100, **Claudia Severa**, wife of a Roman army commander, was living at a fort in Scottish frontier territory. Today she's remembered for the charming birthday party invitation she sent to a friend: 'You'll make the day so much more fun!'

Much more recently, English-born, Scottish-based writer **J K Rowling** (see page 213) has made her home in Scotland. So has Swedish **Sigrid Rausing** (b 1962), heir to a vast industrial fortune, who campaigns to preserve the Scottish wilderness and supports Scottish conservation charities.

Legally speaking:

- A Scot is anyone living in Scotland and named on the register of electors; parentage, ethnic origin or upbringing do not matter.
- In the most recent UK Census (2011) 62% of Scottish residents identified themselves as 'purely Scottish' rather than 'Scottish and British'.
- There is presently no Scottish citizenship; Scots are legally Britons. Although, post-Brexit, that may change…

Image and reality

In spite of government rules that define Scottish identity, traditional Scottish stereotypes are still alive and kicking. They mostly feature Scottish men – wearing kilts, drinking whisky, playing bagpipes, making aggressive gestures, or looking manly, muscular and moody in the Scottish countryside.

But what about the women? In popular presentation, Scottish females have tended to fall into just three categories:

- the flame-haired temptress wearing a flattering but unrealistic mock-traditional costume
- the shy, fey, wistful 'natural' beauty in a wild, romantic setting; the more heather, bluebells or seashore waves, the better
- the hard-working, strong-minded, straight-talking matriarch.

Such images of traditional Scots females are everywhere. But information about real Scottish women from the past is not so easy to find. And when we do come across it, the truth is often very much stranger – and much, much more tragic – than fiction.

'The worst of all'

It can be very difficult to find out about poor Scottish women from the past. But, occasionally, records kept by national and local government officials allow us to 'meet' women such as **Mary Gilmour**. At any time, countless women and girls like her were only weeks away from misery and starvation.

In 1851, Mary, aged eighteen, unwell, out of work, with no family to help her and abandoned by her boyfriend, was found by a Poor Relief inspector. She was sharing Glasgow lodgings with an equally wretched older woman and a young, blind child.

'This is the worst of all the bad habitations I ever saw – A Cellar – earth floor, joist roof – unfit for pigs – neither stool nor aught else. Applicant [Mary] huddled amongst straw in a recess... scarcely long enough for a child to lay in – Her clothes gone [exchanged] for food – she is naked. ... She wrought [worked] in Port Eglinton Mill till within the last 4 weeks & was compelled to give up her situation on acct [account] of ill health...'*

* *From Esther Breitenbach,* Scottish Women, A Documentary History 1780–1914, *Edinburgh University Press 2013, page 93.*

Hidden from history

Today, it seems amazing to recall that until recently women's history was a new and rather suspect branch of study. The lives of women in the past were not thought to have been important. Compared with men, past women had little political, economic or legal power; their lives were private, not public. Women's achievements – in the home, behind the scenes – were often not valued or remembered.

In this book, we will look at the lives and careers of Scottish women mostly from past centuries, but also including some still alive today. The majority of them will have done good, in one way or another, but some won fame and even fortune through deliberate dark deeds. Others were simply foolish, or tragic victims. We will also consider the remarkable achievements of just a few bold and resourceful Scottish women who left to live and work in far-flung regions. Where would we be without them?

Home and away - Scottish women abroad

From around 1700 to the early twentieth century, many thousands of poor women from the Highlands and Lowlands left Scotland in search of better prospects overseas. Their individual lives were not well-documented. We do, however, know a little more about a few remarkable Scottish women overseas:

- Hekja (born c AD 995), a Viking woman slave from Scotland. Brought to Vinland (now Newfoundland) by Viking voyager Leif Erikson around 1010. Perhaps the first Scottish woman in America?

- Elizabeth Macquarie (1788–1835) Gave diplomatic support to her husband, controversial Governor of the New South Wales prison colony in Australia. Planned new roads, designed gardens, promoted farming, went on expeditions to explore and worked for the welfare of women convicts.

- Fanny Inglis, Marquesa Calderón de la Barca (1804–1882) Born in Edinburgh, moved to France, then the USA. Married a Spanish diplomat; lived with him in Mexico. Described the country and people – especially women and girls – in books, letters and journals, creating an invaluable record for future historians.

- Jennie Trout (1841–1921) Born in the Scottish Borders, emigrated to Canada. Worked as a teacher then trained as a doctor. Canada's first licensed woman physician.

- Margaret Graham (1860–1933) Born in Orkney, became a medical missionary and devoted her working life to disadvantaged peoples in Nigeria. Buried next to Mary Slessor (see page 140).

- Lady Evelyn Cobbold (1867–1963). Intrepid traveller; from Edinburgh, she explored deserts in Egypt and Libya. Became a Muslim; one of the first-ever Scottish women to make the Hajj (pilgrimage to Mecca, Arabia).

- Janet Fraser (1883–1945) From Glasgow. Pioneer campaigner for women's rights and social justice in New Zealand. Also active in government as a team with her husband, the Prime Minister.

- Mary Young (1883–1945) From Aberdeen, made a career in France as a nurse. During

World War II, sheltered British secret agents working with the French Resistance. Captured by German troops and sent to Ravensbruck concentration camp, where she died.

- Flora Shaw Stewart (1886–1979) Born near Edinburgh, emigrated to Australia then Papua New Guinea. Mined for gold, kept race-horses, shot crocodiles and ran a hotel. Known as 'Ma', she ruled over rowdy miners and explorers, keeping their treasures under her bed – the 'safest place in town'.

Words about women

For centuries before print media, information and ideas were passed on by Scottish 'keepers of tradition'. Most were women. Their ballads, songs and stories created a vivid imaginary world, largely unknown to men. The songs were entertainments, but also histories, remembering past people and events, and warnings, about everything from dangerous places to dastardly seducers. And they let women escape to an exciting realm where the rules of normal life did not apply.

Here is part of the 'Ballad of Tam Lin', collected by **Agnes Gordon** (1747–1810):

Janet goes to a haunted well and picks flowers. Young, handsome Tam Lin appears; she defies him. Soon Janet is pregnant. Her father is angry. Janet hurries back to the well, where Tam Lin explains: the Queen of the Fairies has carried him away.

'Gloomy, gloomy was the night, And eerie was the way…'. But bravely, Janet waits for

the fairies to ride by, sees Tam Lin, pulls him
from his horse, AND THEN:

'They'll turn me in your arms, lady,
Into an esk and adder;
But hold me fast, and fear me not,
I am your bairn's father.'

'They'll turn me to a bear sae grim,
And then a lion bold;
But hold me fast, and fear me not,
As ye shall love your child.'

'Again they'll turn me in your arms
To a red het gaud of airn [bar of iron];
But hold me fast, and fear me not,
I'll do to you nae harm.'

'And last they'll turn me in your arms
Into the burning gleed [coal];
Then throw me into well water,
O throw me in wi speed.'

'And then I'll be your ain true-love,
I'll turn a naked knight;
Then cover me wi your green mantle,
And cover me out o sight.'

Janet stays faithful. What a woman!

> **En ma Fin git mon Commencement...**
>
> *(Old French: 'In my end is my beginning...')*

Remarkably prescient words embroidered by Mary Queen of Scots shortly before she was executed, in England, in 1587

> **She has withal an alluring grace, a pretty Scotch accent, and a searching wit, clouded with mildness. Fame might move some to relieve her and glory joined with gain might stir others to adventure much for her sake.**

English government secret agent, about Mary Queen of Scots, c 1570–1580

CHAPTER ONE

A SCOTTISH FAMOUS FIVE

Where else to begin this book but with the five Scottish women that almost everyone has heard of: Mary Queen of Scots, Flora MacDonald, St Margaret, Queen Elizabeth the Queen Mother and Scotland's First Minister herself, Nicola Sturgeon. This chapter will be about them.

Of course many other Scottish women certainly deserve their fame: brilliant scientists Mary Somerville and Williamina Fleming. Pioneer doctors James Barry and Elsie Inglis. Humanitarian Mary Slessor. And social justice campaigner Fanny Wright. Let's not forget Jacobite rebels 'Colonel' Anne MacIntosh and Jenny Cameron, to say nothing of strange, brilliant artist Margaret MacDonald and formidable sports mother Judy Murray. And sharp, sour novelist Muriel Spark. And brilliant pathologist Professor Dame Susan Black. And nine-year-old Suffragette Bessie Watson. And school student Amal Azzudin, who together with her classmates 'the Glasgow Girls' protested against inhumane treatment of asylum-seekers. And more, and more – a splendid procession, from Scotland's remote past right up to today. All these will appear later in the book. Read on and find out more.

Mary, Mary quite contrary

A very controversial figure, **Mary Queen of Scots** 'got her head chopped off' in 1587. What had she done wrong? Was she a 'mermaid' (prostitute), as the Edinburgh mob alleged? Was she a martyr to her Roman Catholic faith at a time of strident Scottish Protestantism, as later supporters have claimed? Or was she simply a victim of history: the wrong woman in the wrong place at the wrong time?

Mary was born in 1542, just a few days after her father, Scotland's King James V, died, probably from dysentery though more romantic writers say the cause was a broken heart. James had just been defeated – disastrously – in battle by English troops at Solway Moss, in the Borders. His kingdom was poor, weak and bullied by a stronger neighbour. He himself was still young (only thirty) and personally attractive, but he had failed to stop feuds between power-hungry Scottish nobles and bloody quarrels among rival religious factions. Both threatened to tear Scotland apart. And, although he had at least nine children born out of wedlock, James had failed to father a surviving royal son.

Scotland at that time was not an easy place for anyone to rule, let alone a baby. In 1543, when Mary was just ten months old, King Henry VIII launched a take-over bid, 'packaged' as a marriage proposal from his infant son, Prince Edward. Mary's mother, Marie of Guise (see page 55) and her supporters among Scots nobles said 'No!'. In reply, King Henry launched a series of invasions, cruelly nicknamed 'the Rough Wooing'.

For safety, young Mary (now almost six) was sent away to France, her mother's homeland and the strongest, richest kingdom in Europe. A new marriage alliance was planned, this time to the French Dauphin (Crown Prince). Mary was a delightful child – clever, well-behaved, quick to learn, graceful, pretty, musical, keen on outdoor sports and also skilled at typically female accomplishments such as embroidery. The poor Dauphin was weak, sickly and bad-tempered, but they grew fond of each other. In 1558, when Mary was fifteen, they married in a splendid ceremony. The next year, after the Dauphin's father died, they became king and queen of France.

However, just one year later (1560), Mary's hopes for a happy future in France were dashed. Her husband died. The French did not want her. She was sent back to Scotland. To Mary, Scotland was by now a foreign country. (For years, she had spoken, thought and even dreamed in French.) She did not understand the Scots, and they did not understand her. She was too ignorant, too inexperienced, too emotionally unstable and – for many – too Catholic to be Scotland's queen. That same year, the Scottish Parliament voted to make Scotland Protestant. And she was a woman, weak (so people said) and dangerously beautiful.

Mary's brief reign in Scotland (1560–1568) sometimes reads like the plot of a particularly lurid novel: foolish choices, headstrong love, riot, rape, kidnap and murder. Did Mary bring disaster on herself? Was she manipulated by other, more wily politicians? Did she lack the tact and patience that had helped her mother rule so well? Or did she simply not know enough about Scotland and how its government worked? The answer is probably a mixture of all these reasons.

The (very) sorry tale begins with a marriage. As queen, it was Mary's duty to wed and produce heirs. For her husband, Mary chose a distant cousin from a Catholic family, tall, handsome, vicious, unreliable Henry Darnley. Scottish Protestants were furious, and rioted.

The romance did not last long. Darnley was unfaithful and jealous – of Mary's position as queen, and of her private secretary, Italian

David Rizzio. As Mary and Rizzio enjoyed a quiet musical evening at Edinburgh's Holyrood Palace, Darnley's men dragged him away and stabbed him fifty-six times.

Mary's (and Darnley's) son – the future King James VI of Scotland / James I of England – was born soon after, in 1566. Mary could not forgive Darnley for Rizzio's murder, or for his increasingly wild and dissolute lifestyle. Unwisely, she sought advice from another ill-advised companion, Scotland's violent, philandering High Admiral James Hepburn, Earl of Bothwell.

In 1567, the house where Darnley had been staying was demolished in an explosion. Darnley's body was found in the garden. He had been strangled before the blast. Bothwell was suspected, but not convicted. It was also rumoured that he and Mary were lovers. Just two months after Darnley died, Mary seems to have agreed to be 'kidnapped' and 'raped' by Bothwell, perhaps to hide the fact that she was already pregnant. (She later gave birth to very premature twins, who died.) Then Mary and Bothwell wed.

Enough was enough. In June 1567, Scottish Protestant nobles rebelled. Bothwell fled to Denmark (where he later died, insane). Captive, Mary was taken to Edinburgh and forced to abdicate. Her baby son became king. Mary spent the next year as a prisoner in Loch Leven castle, then escaped and fled to England, where she hoped her cousin Queen Elizabeth I would help her. However, to Elizabeth, Mary was a threat, not a queenly ally. She kept Mary under (fairly) comfortable house arrest for almost twenty years. But Mary became a focus of plots by Elizabeth's enemies and by English Catholics. Reluctantly, in 1587, Elizabeth decided that it was too dangerous to let Mary live.

Mary's end was as dramatic as her life had been. She climbed on to the scaffold dressed in red, the colour of blood (and of martyrdom). And then, when the axeman picked up her freshly-severed head, it left him clutching at an auburn wig, and handfuls of thin air…

Pearly queen

Half Anglo-Saxon and half Ukrainian / Russian / Swedish (and not setting foot on Scottish soil until she was over twenty), saintly **Queen Margaret** (1045–1093) is nonetheless remembered as 'The Pearl* of Scotland' – and was the first Scottish woman officially to be named as queen (rather than just wife-of-the-king). A right royal mixture of bloodlines and cultures, like members of most ruling families in medieval Europe, Margaret's life story was recorded by admiring Christian chroniclers, who held her up as a shining example of super-devout womanhood. Because of this, it is almost impossible to discover what the 'real' Margaret was like. Even so, we can see that she clearly was a remarkable woman, educated, principled and determined.

This much we do know: Margaret was born in Hungary around 1045. Her parents were Anglo-Saxon Prince Edward the Exile and Princess Agatha, who was probably the daughter of Yaroslav the Wise of Kiev,

* *The name Margaret comes from a Greek word meaning pearl.*

although she might just possibly have been Polish or even Bulgarian. Margaret's father was heir to the throne of England. But he had been smuggled away to mainland Europe after Danish Vikings conquered his father's kingdom. He eventually found refuge at the court of St Stephen of Hungary, and met and married Agatha. Margaret was born there.

Margaret spent the first years of her life in Hungary, then returned with her father and the rest of her family to England in 1057, where the Anglo-Saxon king planned to make Edward the Exile his heir. But Edward died soon after he reached England. His widow and children (including Margaret) stayed on at the English royal court.

In 1066, the Normans invaded England, and their leader William the Conqueror became king. Fearing for their safety, Agatha decided to take her children – all now young adults – back to eastern Europe. In 1068, they travelled north to escape the advancing Normans, then boarded a ship to cross the North Sea. But it was stormy weather and the ship was blown off course. It finally limped into sheltered waters off the east coast of Scotland, not far from Dunfermline, close to a headland known today as St Margaret's Hope.

Margaret was young, royal, well-educated, brave; according to the chroniclers, she was beautiful, as well. So, dear readers, would you like the romantic version of what happened next, or the (so far as we know) more realistic one? For centuries, legends and paintings have shown demure, smiling, elegantly-dressed Margaret being welcomed at the quayside by Scotland's King Malcolm III, who is clearly overwhelmed by his feelings. It's love at first sight! Much more probably, Margaret and her family, cold, wet and shivering, would have been apprehended by wary Scottish officials. Maybe they were even locked up for a while, until their identity could be proven and valuables they had brought with them had been handed over to provide more comfortable accommodation.

In real life, Margaret may not have got to know King Malcolm until 1070. But by 1072, at the latest, they were married. They were an unlikely couple. Margaret probably wanted to be a nun; Malcolm was older, a widower, and a brutal warrior; he had killed Macbeth to gain the throne. He could not read or write and had little time for religion. The marriage was political – Margaret was a living link with the last Anglo-Saxon kings and union with her would strengthen Malcolm's power.

Best behaviour!

The Scottish royal court was famously uncivilised, more like a soldiers' mess than a splendid symbol of Scotland. Margaret decided to change all that, and, amazingly, succeeded.

Margaret's rules! Visitors must be:

- clean and washed – not dirty and smelly

- neatly and decently dressed

- polite and respectful

- peaceable – guests must not trash the (new, fine) furnishings, or fight and kill each other!

Mother of a nation

As a royal wife, Margaret did very well. She gave birth to eight children (six boys, two girls) and closely supervised their education, bringing learned, religious teachers to the royal court. Three of her sons became kings of Scotland; a fourth shared royal power; a fifth became head of a great monastery; the sixth died in battle fighting alongside his father. One of her daughters became Queen of England (see page 64); the other married a leading Crusader nobleman in France.

As a proud, defiant sign of Margaret's Anglo-Saxon and European heritage and / or of her faith, her children were almost all given English (or biblical) names: Edward, Edmund, Ethelred, Edgar, Alexander, Edith, Mary and David. These had not been used for Scottish royalty before.

Although her husband and children were important to her, Margaret's greatest love seems to have been the Christian religion. It was said that she got up every night at midnight, to attend church services; she spent hours on her knees in a damp, dark cave, saying prayers. She read holy books to herself – and out loud to King Malcolm. For her sake, he listened, and he paid for the books to be given jewelled covers because he knew it would please her. Margaret also gave to charity – it was said she fed twenty poor babies every day, using a golden spoon. She washed the feet of beggars. She built new churches and monasteries. She also paid for a new ferry (still called Queensferry, near Edinburgh) to help pilgrims reach the shrine of St Andrew in Fife. She brought Church scholars to help run the Scottish government, and to change old, Celtic ways of Christian worship to the latest European style.

Losing her head

Margaret was made a saint in 1250. Her body was embalmed and revered as a precious relic. Centuries later, the head was moved to a resting place of honour in Edinburgh Castle, where Margaret's descendant, Mary Queen of Scots, claimed that it protected her. After Mary's execution, the head was taken for safety to a monastery in France. It disappeared, probably destroyed, during the French Revolution, c 1789.

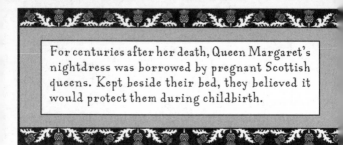

For centuries after her death, Queen Margaret's nightdress was borrowed by pregnant Scottish queens. Kept beside their bed, they believed it would protect them during childbirth.

Margaret died in her late forties, just three days after hearing that King Malcolm and their oldest son had been killed fighting the English. People said that her heart was broken – and that as her coffin passed her husband's grave it mysteriously became too heavy to move and so they had to be buried together.

flower of Scotland?

'Bonnie Charlie's noo awa…' Yes, he is, and we all know who helped him escape: **Flora MacDonald** (1722–1790).

In 1746, the last Jacobite uprising was defeated. (Jacobites were supporters of King James VII of Scotland / King James II of England, who fled into exile in 1688. His descendants claimed the Scottish and English thrones, which were united when Scotland joined England as a single kingdom in 1707.)

The last Jacobite leader, 'Bonnie Prince Charlie', fled across the sea to the island of Benbecula in the Outer Hebrides.

In 1746, Flora MacDonald, aged twenty-three and from the Isle of Skye, was visiting her brother who lived on Benbecula.

Bonnie Charlie's noo awa

Bonnie Charlie's noo awa
Safely o'er the friendly main [sea]
He'rts will a'most break in twa'
Should he ne'er come back again.

Chorus
Will ye no' come back again?
Will ye no' come back again?
Better lo'ed [loved] ye canna be
Will ye no' come back again?

Lyrics: Scottish poet Carolina Oliphant, Lady Nairne, 1766–1845. From a Jacobite family, her poems were very popular but have been described as 'saccharine'.

Tune: Traditional Scottish

Pro-English volunteer soldiers were on patrol nearby. Another of Flora's relatives, Captain Con O'Neill, was one of Charles's aides. He asked Flora to help them. So Flora and her servants disguised Prince Charles as 'muckle carlin'* Irish serving maid 'Betty Burke' (Charles was over 1.8 metres (6 feet) tall). The disguise was unconvincing – one of Flora's friends complained that it made Charles more conspicuous, not less – but Flora persuaded sailors to take Charles across the sea to her step-father's home on Skye. After further adventures, a French warship arrived to carry Charles away from Scotland, for ever.

The boatmen were arrested and interrogated. Flora was arrested, too, and taken to the Tower of London. After several months, in 1747 she was released on parole, and sent to live with the wife of an English Government supporter in London. Many people from polite society came to meet her, including the Prince of Wales. She made a favourable impression. Famous author Samuel Johnson described her as 'a woman of soft features, gentle manners, kind soul and elegant presence'.

* *Big old woman.*

In 1750, Flora returned to Skye to marry a captain in the English army. But times were tough in the Highlands and Islands. In 1774, like many other Scots, Flora and her family emigrated to America, where her husband and her five sons fought on the British side against rebels demanding independence for the USA. When Flora's husband was taken prisoner, for safety she sailed back to Skye, where she died in 1790.

Clearly, a life well-lived. But never, in all her days, did Flora claim to be a Jacobite supporter, let alone a Jacobite heroine. When asked why she had helped Prince Charles escape, her reply was simple: 'Out of charity, as I would have helped anyone defeated and in distress.'

Canny granny

'Her Majesty, the last Empress of India.' The 'most dangerous woman in England' (Adolf Hitler). A 'steel marshmallow' (society photographer Cecil Beaton). Or a 'pretty, comfy, walking sofa...'? (cultural commentators Anne Barr and Peter York).

Whatever people said about her – and all four of the above remarks reflect aspects of her personality – everyone agreed that **Elizabeth Angela Marguerite Bowes-Lyon** (1900–2002), later Her Majesty Queen Elizabeth the Queen Mother ('the Queen Mum'), had charm. Lots and lots of charm. Petite, plump and pretty, lively, witty, always gracious and almost always smiling (the first British royal to do so in public!), Elizabeth spent eighty years in the spotlight, and was the longest-living member of the British royal family when she died in 2002, aged 101.

The ninth (out of ten) children of a Scottish nobleman, Elizabeth was born in England, but spent long periods of her childhood in one of

her family's two stately homes, fairytale Glamis
Castle, near Forfar in Scotland. Riding, playing
with dogs and other country sports were her
favourite pastimes; she was not a great scholar.
As a teenager during the 1914–1918 War, she
helped care for wounded soldiers lodging at
the castle. She was capable, cheery and, yes,
charming.

In her early twenties, Elizabeth famously
rejected two marriage proposals from 'Bertie',
duke of York. She said this was because she
feared that as a member of the royal family
she would never be free to be herself. (Others
unkindly muttered that it was because she
would have preferred to marry a more
important royal – the Prince of Wales.) At
last, she accepted Bertie's third proposal, and
settled down to a life of happy, conventional
domesticity, wealth and privilege. Bertie was a
kind and thoughtful man, and they grew to be a
devoted couple. Their cosy, comfortable world
was shattered by the scandalous abdication
crisis of 1936, when Bertie's older brother,
now King Edward VIII, gave up the throne to
marry his American mistress, Wallis Simpson,
and Bertie became king, as George VI.

Sisters-in-law Elizabeth and Wallis did not get on. Elizabeth blamed Wallis – 'that woman' –for Bertie's early death after World War II, brought on, she alleged, by the strain of royal duties. In return, Wallis gave Elizabeth the nickname 'Cookie', saying that she was fat and common, like a domestic servant. No-one came out of the situation well, and the royal family's reputation was badly damaged. It was salvaged, somewhat, by Bertie's – and Elizabeth's – bravery during World War II. As Hitler judged, correctly, the royal couple became inspirational leaders, refusing to leave

Elizabeth in wartime

'The children won't go [leave Britain] without me. I won't leave the King. And the King will never leave.'

'I'm glad we've [Buckingham Palace] been bombed. It makes me feel I can look the East End* in the face.'

* The East End of London, a very poor district, suffered terribly from wartime bombing.

London during the worst bombing raids, tirelessly visiting troops, hospitals and bomb-shelters, and providing an image of steadfast, loving family life that people in wartime Britain could identify with.

'Life-enhancer'?

Widowed aged only fifty-one, Elizabeth created a new role for herself, as Queen Mother – a sort of favourite Scottish grandmother to the nation. Grand she certainly was; one obituary called her 'defiantly aristocratic'. She knew her own mind and was not afraid to express old-fashioned, sometimes prejudiced, opinions, but only in private. She spent lavishly and loved fine food and drink, paintings, jewellery, racehorses. She went fishing. She played cards (and liked to win) and party games, and kept sweeties in her handbag, even on state occasions. She bought – and restored – a remote Scottish castle (Mey) as a kind of therapy after Bertie's death. And she stayed loyal and dutiful to her dead husband's ideals, right to the end. Prince Charles knew her better than most; he called her a life-enhancer.

'Nippy sweetie'

It's often said that, together with journalists, politicians are among the least-trusted and admired professionals. So what made **Nicola Ferguson Sturgeon** (b 1970) choose a career – a life – in politics, aged only sixteen? The answer to that question appears at first rather surprising. It was, reportedly, because of Margaret Thatcher. But not because Sturgeon admired Mrs Thatcher's policies – although she has said she believes more women should take part in politics. Rather, Sturgeon said she had a strong feeling that it was wrong for Scotland to be ruled by a government that the Scots hadn't elected.

The political party that Sturgeon joined as soon as she was old enough was the Scottish National Party (SNP). She was following a family example; her mother, Joan, was already an SNP local councillor. Founded in 1934, the SNP had elected Members of Parliament at Westminster since 1967. It has been a prominent force in the Scottish Parliament ever since Devolution in 1999, and has formed the Scottish Government since 2007. Its policies are centre-left, anti-nuclear and pro-European. And, of course, it wants Scottish independence. By 2018, it had become the UK's second largest political party.*

Born to an everyday working family in North Ayrshire, Sturgeon studied law at Glasgow University, then qualified as a solicitor. Her concern for social justice was reflected in her work at a Law Centre in a disadvantaged district of Glasgow, but she became a full-time politician aged only twenty-nine. Today, Sturgeon is not only the first woman to be leader of the SNP, but also First Minister of Scotland.

Determined, cautious, clear-headed and very hard-working, Sturgeon has an excellent rapport with SNP grass-roots supporters, though she can be tough and sharp at times – the Scottish term is 'nippy sweetie'. Like any other politician, her career has had its low points; losing the Scottish Independence Referendum in 2014 (she had led the SNP campaign) was a severe disappointment.

* Only the London-based Labour Party is larger.

Today, Sturgeon faces her biggest challenges so far: how to secure the best deal for Scotland amid shambolic Brexit negotiations (62% of Scots voted 'Remain'). And even more difficult: when – if ever – to choose the right time to hold another Independence Referendum.

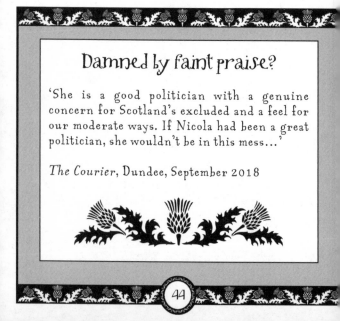

Damned by faint praise?

'She is a good politician with a genuine concern for Scotland's excluded and a feel for our moderate ways. If Nicola had been a great politician, she wouldn't be in this mess...'

The Courier, Dundee, September 2018

'Sonsie'

Another good old Scots word, sonsie (big and bonny) describes the politician who has been Nicola Sturgeon's chief opponent in the Scottish Parliament since 2011. Trained as a journalist, with leadership skills, a ready wit and a genius for positive publicity, **Ruth Davidson** (b 1978) has transformed the fortunes of the Conservative Party in Scotland. Tipped as a possible future leader of the UK-wide Conservatives, for the moment Davidson has said that she regards her task as 'to hold the SNP to account'. (In fact, Davidson and Sturgeon have quite a lot in common. Both are pro-Europe, support immigration and are socially liberal.) The first Scottish Conservative leader to be openly gay, Davidson is currently on maternity leave and has just had her first child – another milestone for the Scottish Parliament.

❝...While Europe's eye is fix'd on mighty things, The fate of empires and the fall of kings; While quacks of State must each produce his plan, And even children lisp the Rights of Man; Amid this mighty fuss just let me mention, The Rights of Woman merit some attention...**❞**

Robert Burns, 1792

Written as an 'Occasional Address' and spoken by one of Burns's favourite actors, Louisa Fontenelle (1769–1799),* in a Dumfries theatre.

Praised for her 'agreeable vivacity', Fontanelle was born in London but spent much of her career in Scotland. She was famous for playing breeches roles, where women took the parts of young men or boys. She married a theatre-manager friend of Robert Burns, and they emigrated to America, where she died of yellow fever aged only thirty.

CHAPTER TWO

MONSTROUS REGIMENT – WOMEN IN POLITICS

J ust three years after the French Revolution, when governments throughout Europe were cracking down hard on the slightest signs of dissent, Burns used his 'Occasional Address' to flirt defiantly and dangerously with the idea of revolutionary rights. Although in his poem, with typical, if sexist, gallantry, Burns defines women's rights as protection, decorum (respect) and admiration, his female speaker is clearly of independent mind and judgement. Like so many other Scottish women, past and present...

We cannot prove it, of course, but it would be surprising if there had not been politically-powerful women in Scotland since the time that the first post-Ice Age settlers splashed their way across the shallow North Sea over 10,000 years ago, or, about 5,000 years later, braved the waves between Spain and the western British Isles. It took toughness and determination to face – and survive – the journey into the unknown. Yet, although much remains hidden, some of the earliest writings about Scotland do provide tantalising glimpses.

Sgathaich

An awesome presence in the Ulster Cycle of myths, Sgathaich was said to live in a mountain-top 'Fortress of Shadows', perhaps the Cuillin ridge on Skye. She taught Irish (male) hero Cu Chulainn how to fight, and gave him a deadly barbed spear, the gae bolga.

At first into myth, where we learn about warrior princesses such as **Sgathaich** and her sister and rival **Aife**, whose power lay in strange, sinister magic...

The creatures of Scottish folklore are also often female, with powers of peculiar – sometimes terrifying – kinds. Here are just a few:

- Selkies – mysterious, beautiful seal-women, who marry humans, then return to the sea, leaving their spouses broken-hearted.

- Glastaigs – half woman, half goat and green! They protect farm animals – or destroy them.

- Loch monsters – not just Nessie, but also Morag, from Loch Morar. There are others, as well: all are as perilous as the deep waters where they live.

- Cailleach Bheur – the spirit of winter, old age and cold, dark fear. She'll freeze the life out of anything.

And what are we to make of accounts by early chroniclers, on both sides of the Irish Sea, of a female giant washed up on a beach in Scotland around AD 900? Reportedly, she was almost 60 m (195 ft) tall, with amazingly long (5.5 m / 18 feet) hair.

These powerful, mythical women may be 'humanised' goddesses, not fragments of history. The monsters may embody deep-seated fears. But perfectly sane and rational Roman writers described strong women leaders among the Celtic tribes they fought against. And, over 1,000 years after the mythic stories took shape, Icelandic Sagas describe the activities of (probably real) Norse women who lived some time between AD 800–1100.

Archaeological findings also suggest the existence of respected prehistoric women. For example, the remains of '**Ava**', a member of a farming community who died around 4200 BC in Achavanich, Caithness, were buried in a chamber painstakingly carved out of solid rock, which must have taken weeks or months to create. A fine pottery vessel, filled with medicinal herbs and flowers, had been placed beside the body. Ava herself had a strangely-shaped skull, perhaps produced by deliberate moulding.

Together, these three pieces of evidence tell us that Ava was of particular importance to the people surrounding her. After all, the dead do not bury themselves – someone else has to choose what to do and how to do it. Ava was young (probably between eighteen and twenty-two). So was her significance hereditary; was she from a powerful family? Or did she have some other valued status, as a priestess or shaman, maybe?

Aud the Deep-Minded
(c AD 850)

Daughter and then widow of Norse warlords in Scotland, **Aud** ordered a new ship to be built and led her kinsfolk from Caithness to Orkney, then across stormy northern seas to settle in the 'unknown' territory of Iceland. She steered the ship herself. Wise and dignified, she divided the land among the settlers and ruled well. She was given a Viking hero's burial.

Recent surveys of women's graves in Viking-era Scotland (c AD 800–1200) have also discovered that they are richer and much more numerous than elsewhere in the British Isles. Does this mean that the Scottish women buried there had high status in their communities – maybe higher than men? For example, a Viking grave at Scarr in Orkney contains the remains of an unusually elderly woman (about seventy years old), a male warrior and her young child. Was she a powerful person? Was the man her bodyguard? Was the child her servant or companion for the next world? It is possible.

There have even been suggestions that the rich 'warrior' grave discovered recently (2011) in Ardnamurchan – the first intact Viking ship burial ever unearthed on the UK mainland – may have been a high-ranking, powerful woman. It contains tools typically used by Viking women, and also a ritually-misshapen spear and a sword: symbols of power.

Princess Scota

Medieval history writers mixed myth and legend with fact and memory. **Princess Scota** may not have existed, but she symbolised a whole people.* She appears in early texts such as the *Scotichronicon* (c AD 1440); all tell different versions of her story. Some say she was the Egyptian wife of an Ancient Greek prince. Banished, they fled to Spain. From there, one of their sons sailed to Ireland then Scotland, which he named in honour of his mother. Other legends tell how an unnamed Egyptian wed the King of Portugal; Scota was their daughter. She married the King of Ireland, and their sons invaded Scotland. The invaders called themselves 'Children of Scota' and gave their name to the country.

It was also sometimes said that Scota carried a giant stone slab with her from the Middle East. A huge stone was used in Scottish coronation ceremonies. It still exists and is known as the Stone of Destiny. But it weighs over 150 kg, and when it was stolen by Scottish Nationalists in 1950 it took three strong men to move it. Scota must have been a wonder-woman!

* *'Scoti' was the name given by Roman writers to pirates who raided the north-western British Isles. It was probably the Roman version of a Celtic word meaning 'sail'.*

Unsex me here!

Perhaps the most formidable woman in politics from Scotland's distant past is **Lady Macbeth**, at least as she is portrayed in Shakespeare's play. Named **Gruoch ingen Boite**,* the real Lady Macbeth lived from around 1020–1054. Apart from the fact that she gave generously to a Christian monastery, we know little about her. Macbeth was her second husband; her first had been gruesomely killed by enemies. As the grand-daughter of a king, Gruoch would have been familiar with palace politics. Perhaps, like most royal women in past times, she encouraged and advised her husband. Perhaps she consulted witches. More than that, we cannot say.

However, in Shakespeare's play, Gruoch is at the very heart of the story. She, not Macbeth, is the one filled with driving ambition. She wants to be queen; she wants political and military power for herself, as well as for her husband. She's bold, daring, opportunist, cruel, immoral and above all, 'unwomanly'. She suppresses all her 'feminine' qualities to get what she wants.

* *Gruoch, daughter of Bodhe, a prince in north-east Scotland.*

In other words, in Shakespeare's text, Lady Macbeth symbolises all that has been considered problematic over the centuries about women and power. (And she's punished for it – she loses her mind, suffers agonies of remorse and eventually commits suicide.) Shakespeare was not alone in his concerns. They persisted, backed up by laws, until the twentieth century. In words and deeds, Scottish women have had to struggle to overcome them.

Against nature

In 1558, around fifty years before Shakespeare created 'The Scottish Play', an even more outspoken attack on women with power – 'The First Blast of the Trumpet against the Monstrous Regiment of Women' – was published by fiercely Protestant Scottish preacher John Knox. It was an attack on not one but two female rulers: Queen Marie of Guise, widow of King James V, who ruled Scotland on behalf of her young daughter Mary Queen of Scots, and Queen Mary Tudor of England.

Of course, Knox was not blasting his trumpet against imaginary ranks of Scottish female soldiers. No, he was insisting that a 'regiment' – a regime, any regime – headed by a woman was monstrous, against God and nature, abnormal, an outrage, just plain wrong. Even – especially – in Scotland.

Weel, that's us tell't, then...

'For who can denie but it repugneth to nature, that the blind shal be appointed to leade and conduct [guide] such as do see? That the weake, the sicke, and impotent persones shall norishe and kepe [protect] the hole and strong, and finallie, that the foolishe, madde and phrenetike [frenzied] shal governe the discrete, and give counsel to such as be sober of mind? And such be all women, compared vnto man in bearing of authoritie. For their sight in civile regiment [government], is but blindnes: their strength, weaknes: their counsel, foolishenes: and judgement, phrenesie [frenzy]...'

John Knox, 1558

'A woman with a man's courage'

Although **Marie (or Mary) of Guise** (1515–1560), the target of Knox's 'blast', is often overshadowed by her far more glamorous daughter, she was an admirable ruler in very difficult times. She was born to an ambitious French noble family who intended her to be a nun. However, her parents removed Marie from the convent when they saw what attractive marriage-market material she was growing up to be. Marie was tall and well-built (good for childbearing, sixteenth-century people said – a wife's main duty was to produce an heir), intelligent, conscientious, with gracious manners, a fine complexion and pretty dark-red hair.

Aged eighteen, Marie married a French duke, who turned down other possible brides because she impressed him so much. Alas, their happiness did not last long. Less than three years after the wedding, the Duke died, leaving Marie pregnant with their second son, who did not survive. Marie treasured the last letter he wrote to her for the rest of her life.

Soon, Marie's family negotiated another marriage, this time to James V, King of Scotland. Marie was reluctant to leave France and her only surviving son for cold, 'uncivilised' Scotland and an unknown bridegroom, but her father insisted. Dutifully, Marie sailed to her new kingdom in 1538, where she impressed James (and his mother and many surly Scottish nobles) with her charm, tact and diplomatic skills.

At first, Marie played no part in politics. In four years, she produced three more children, though the first two (both boys) died. But then her youngest child, Mary, became Queen of Scots aged just eight days old, when King James V died suddenly in 1542.

For the rest of her life, Marie worked tirelessly to keep the kingdom of Scotland united and peaceful, despite power-hungry rival nobles, invading armies sent by Henry VIII of England, and bitter religious quarrels between Scottish Catholics and Protestants. She helped support the war-damaged Scottish economy by arranging aid from France.

Mother love

For a queen long ago, Marie was also remarkably involved with the upbringing of her children. Although they were both far away in France – Mary Queen of Scots was sent to the French royal court for safety, aged five – Marie wrote to them often and anxiously, sending love, guidance and good advice.

Queen Marie of Guise died aged only forty, in 1560. Although she failed in her greatest political ambition, which was to unite Scotland with her beloved homeland, France, she devoted her life to her daughter's kingdom. Few – if any – other Scots at that time would have managed it as well; most would have done far worse. Even Marie's English enemies admired her, describing her as 'a woman with a man's courage'. Well, yes, she was brave – but it was also her 'feminine' tact, patience and tolerance that helped her rule so well.

WORDS ABOUT WOMEN

The Power of Love

For years, Scotland's young King James I (reigned 1406-1437) was held hostage in an English castle. It was grand, and (for the time) comfortable, but still a prison. To distract himself, James read the latest verses, romances, and faibleaux, and tried his hand, with some considerable success, at writing poetry. In his most famous work, 'The Kingis Qhair' (The King's Book), teenage James describes looking out of his tower window and falling in love at first sight with young English noblewoman, Lady Joan Beaufort:

...And therewith kest I doun myn eye ageyne
Whare as I saw walking under the Toure
Full secretly, comyn hir to playne
The fairest or the freschest younge floure
That ever I saw, methought, before that houre,
For which sodayne abate, anon astert
The blude of all my body to my hert.
And though I stood abaisit tho a lyte,
No wonder was; for why? My wytts all
Were so ouercome with pleasance and delyte
Only through latting of myn eyen fall

That suddaynly my heart became hir thrall
For ever of free wyll, for of manace
There was no takyn in her suete face...

The Kingis Quair c 1424

Translation:

And then I looked down again / and saw walking, below the tower / privately, to ease her worries / the fairest or the freshest young flower / which I had ever seen in all my life. / A sudden feeling of weakness / sent all the blood in my body rushing to my heart.

For a while, I was in a bit of a daze / And no wonder – all my wits / were so overcome with pleasure and delight / just by looking at her / my heart had suddenly become her prisoner / for ever, and freely, because there was no sign of menace in her sweet face.

King James and Joan Beaufort married in 1424. The marriage was partly political; the King of England wanted King James to make an alliance with his own country, rather than Scotland's traditional supporter, France. Joan was a close relative of the English king. But James really had been smitten by Joan's beauty. She came from a famously handsome family; her grandmother, another Joan, had been admired throughout Europe as 'the Fair Maid of Kent'.

And yes, they did live happily ever after, and had eight children – until James was murdered in 1437. During the attack, Joan tried to protect her husband, but was badly wounded.

After this, the loving story changes. Joan became guardian of their six-year old son, now King James II – and vowed to avenge her husband's death. Her supporters hunted down King James's assassins and tortured them before executing them – on Joan's orders, it was said. The murderous ringleader, King James's uncle, the Earl of Atholl, was barbarously 'crowned' with a circle of red-hot iron, allegedly inscribed with the words 'the king of traitors'.

Two years later, in 1439, Joan married again. Her new husband was the romantically-titled

'Black Knight of Lorne', but warfare is not romantic and the couple were soon entangled in bitter, bloody struggles between rival Scottish nobles. Young King James II was taken away from Joan, and held under house arrest by her enemies. Joan spent the last year of her life, with her husband and their three children, as a prisoner in Dunbar, and died there aged forty-one in 1445 after enduring a long, grim siege.

A dangerous game

Few wives, mothers or daughters of rulers faced such daunting challenges as Marie of Guise, but many other women did play a part in Scottish politics in the distant past. Some won praise for their efforts, but many fell foul of male power – or male prejudice. Here's a small selection.

- Iurminburg, lived around AD 675, wife of Ecgfrith, King of the Angles in southern Scotland. She dared to oppose powerful Church leaders. In return, they accused her of shooting 'poisoned arrows of speech' into the King's heart.

- Finella, daughter of the Earl of Angus (lived around AD 995). Scottish King Cináed II killed Finella's son. In revenge, Finella ordered a splendid statue of Cináed to be made, and invited him to admire it. But the statue was a trap – as the King came close, it fired spikes into him and killed him. But Finella still grieved for her son.

- An untypical force for good, Matilda (aka Edith) of Scotland (died 1118) daughter of Queen and St Margaret (see page 32), married

Henry I of England and became English queen. Well-educated and well-connected (she was in regular close contact with the Pope), she ruled England while her husband was away at war. Her wisdom and gifts to charity helped win respect for the Scottish royal family, as well as the English.

- Margaret, Maid of Norway (1283–1290). Poor little Margaret, sent away from home and family aged seven, to be queen of an unknown land. Granddaughter of Scottish King Alexander III, but born in Norway (Alexander's daughter had married the Norwegian king), little Margaret was his only surviving heir. Sadly, she died – reportedly, of a surfeit of sweeties – before ever landing on the Scottish mainland to be crowned queen. Margaret was not to blame, but her untimely death led to decades of fighting between Scottish and English rivals for the throne.

- Black Agnes of Dunbar (died 1369) helped save Scotland's independence by defending Dunbar castle for ten long months against English attackers. Left in command by her noble husband, she organised her soldiers to drop rocks on besieging troops, and sent her maids to sweep the battlements as if war were nothing but a dusty nuisance. However much she (and her loyal servants) suffered hunger, thirst, disease and the threat of starvation, Agnes would not give in. Her soldiers taunted the English, shouting: 'Came I early, came I late, I found Agnes at the gate.'

- Sometimes, just belonging to a powerful family was dangerous. Marjory Bruce (d 1316), daughter of independence hero Robert the Bruce who fought England's Edward I, was for years imprisoned in a cage hung from the walls of Berwick Castle, together with her stepmother, Queen Elizabeth de Burgh (d 1327). Countess Isobel of Fife (d 1314) shared their ordeal. She had become King Edward's enemy after she took over her husband's traditional duty to help crown Robert Bruce as king.

- Margaret Drummond (died 1501), mistress and confidante of King James IV. Sent away when she became pregnant, she was said to have been poisoned soon after, together with her two sisters, so that James would be free to marry a politically-important princess.

- Margaret was not the only Scottish royal mistress to be 'disposed of'; one of King David II's many lovers, Katherine Mortimer (lived 1330s), was murdered; he tried – very hard – to cut all his ties with another, the ambitious Margaret Logie (died 1375), after she meddled dangerously in Scottish politics.

- Janet Douglas, Lady Glamis (died 1537). Member of a powerful family who had kept King James V prisoner when he was young, Janet became the focus of the King's hatred of all the Douglas kin. He accused her of witchcraft and of treason by trying to poison him. Janet was innocent, but was burned alive in Edinburgh after her son and her servants were tortured to provide false evidence against her. It is said her ghost – the Grey Lady – still haunts Glamis castle.

- Elizabeth Gunning, Duchess of Hamilton and (later) of Argyll (lived 1733–1790). Born in genteel poverty to Irish parents, Elizabeth (with her sister) charmed London and Edinburgh with her beauty: she was tall and slender, with dark hair and brilliant eyes. Like many modern celebrities, she became famous for being famous and was more than a little disreputable. She made two spectacular marriages – the first, after a Valentine's Day party where she dazzled a duke – was a scandal: in secret, at midnight, using a curtain ring for a wedding ring. But it was (just!) legal. Later, she joined in her husband's family feuds over important Scottish inheritances, and ended her career as a politically-influential private servant to Queen Charlotte.

- Clementina Walkinshaw (1720–1802). Born to a Jacobite (see page 34) family in Scotland, Clementina nursed Bonnie Prince Charlie when he fell ill near Glasgow. After the Jacobites were defeated and Charles left Scotland, Clementina joined him and lived with him for several years. They had a child, Charlotte, but Charles was drunk, abusive and unfaithful. Clementina and Charlotte took refuge in French convents, then relied on gifts from Charles's relatives in Italy to survive. Charlotte died young, leaving Clementina to raise her children. Clementina's will reveals a kind and thoughtful character: she took great care to provide for all the friends and servants who had helped her during difficult times.

- Jane Maxwell, Duchess of Gordon (1749–1812). Intelligent, daring, wilful and beautiful; helped her husband raise a whole new army regiment and became a close advisor to UK Prime Minister William Pitt; she had a wide circle of politically-active friends. Also interested in the 'agricultural revolution'; pioneered new crops on her husband's family lands. Meanwhile, he left her, to live with his mistress.

Plots and performances – Anna of Denmark (1574–1619)

'A princess both godly and beautiful', **Anna** was the daughter of Danish King Erik II. She married Scotland's King James VI when she was fifteen years old, almost losing her life in stormy seas on the way to the wedding. Her husband-to-be blamed the bad weather on Scottish witches (more about them on pages 156–160). Boldly, he set sail for Scandinavia to 'rescue' Anna, though she was, by that time, safe on shore again. (People said this was the only romantic act in the whole of James VI's rather solemn, scholarly life.)

At first Anna was happy, but fell out with James when their oldest son, Prince Henry, was taken away to live with noble foster-parents. This was a Scottish tradition and also a safety precaution, to prevent the King and the heir to the throne being attacked at the same time. Anna sulked, cried, refused to get out of bed and generally made herself a nuisance. More dangerously, she encouraged plots by rival Scots against the family caring for the young prince, and schemed against powerful courtiers whose support her husband relied on.

James VI's fondness for male 'favourites' was legendary, but he and Anna dutifully produced six more royal children for Scotland. But after that, they lived apart and Anna devoted all her time, money and energy to the arts. She invited top painters, architects, dramatists and musicians to the royal court, and paid for leading actors and dancers to perform there, sometimes, shockingly and scantily-clad, joining in herself. She also passed on her high-handed views of the rights of royalty to her favourite son, later King Charles I of England and Scotland. These may have inspired Charles's quarrels with the English Parliament, and led to the terrible Civil War.

from Protests to Parliament

Getting entangled, happily or not, with powerful men was for many centuries the only way for women to make their voices heard in politics. But from the early 1800s, better education, new radical ideals, the growth of mass industrial employment and cheap print media all gave fresh opportunities for women. But getting access to political power was still not easy. Elsewhere in this book, you can read how women protested and campaigned for workers' welfare, equal treatment with men, and the right to vote.

Meanwhile, other female pioneers from all social classes and with very different ideals worked tirelessly to have their say in male-dominated national and local governments. For example:

- Lavinia Malcolm (1847–1920): Schoolteacher, local councillor and Provost (mayor) of the town of Dollar; the first woman in Scotland to be elected as a civic leader. Strong supporter of women's rights to take part in public life.

- Ann Husband (1852–1929): Humanitarian,

social reformer and local councillor in Dundee. Campaigned to improve attitudes to and services for poor people. Also called for nursery schools, and for free school textbooks and school meals. Demanded votes for women.

- Katherine Stewart Murray, Duchess of Atholl (1874–1960): Conservative Party politician; the first Scottish woman elected to the UK Parliament. Campaigned to improve education. Famously opposed appeasement (peace agreement with Hitler's Germany) before World War II.

- Nannie Wells (1875–1963): Early Scottish Nationalist campaigner. Never elected to government, she was a leading figure in Nationalist political parties, and wrote many newspaper articles calling for an independent Scottish government. She was also active in calling for Scotland to oppose fascist politics throughout Europe in the 1930s.

- Jennie Adamson (1882–1962): Labour Party MP, one of the first working-class women elected to UK Parliament. Campaigned to win respect for motherhood, for child welfare – 'boots for bairns' – and women's rights.

- Clarice Shaw (1883–1946): Sunday School teacher and Labour Party campaigner, Shaw worked for improvements in public health and child welfare. She also called for equal pay and employment conditions for women. She was Scotland's first Labour Party town councillor.

- Nan Hughes(1885–1947): Born in poverty, became Provost (mayor) of the town of Cumnock. Pioneered council housing for workers and other welfare schemes.

- Florence Horsburgh (1889–1969): Unionist (Conservative) Party politician and one of the very first women in the UK to become a (junior) government minister and a privy councillor (advisor to the monarch). Her special areas of expertise were education and children's welfare.

- Alice Cullen (1891–1969): Member of UK Parliament for a very poor part of Glasgow; nicknamed 'Mrs Gorbals'. Campaigned for better housing and healthcare. The first Roman Catholic woman elected as an MP.

- Jean Roberts (1895–1988): Teacher, magistrate and local Independent Labour Party councillor in Glasgow. Shrewd, hard-working and patient, she became City Treasurer and then Glasgow's first woman Lord Provost (Lord Mayor), a position of great responsibility and power.

- Jennie (Baroness) Lee (1904–1988): From a poor miner's family, campaigned for equal opportunities. Elected Labour Party MP in the UK Parliament aged twenty-four; later appointed Minister for the Arts. Greatest achievement was setting up the Open University in 1969. Was wife and advisor to Aneurin Bevan, Labour MP (later Prime Minister) who founded the National Health Service.

- Betty Harvie Anderson (1913–1979): Honoured for work as commander of anti-aircraft troops during World War II; became Conservative Party MP and won respect as Deputy Speaker of the House of Commons. Strongly opposed Scottish Devolution and Independence.

- Priscilla Buchan, Lady Tweedsmuir (1915–1978): Conservative MP and government minister in UK Parliament. Strong supporter of United Nations peace-making after World War II. Expert in international relations.

- Dame Judith Hart (1924–1991): Labour MP with radical left-wing views. Campaigned on behalf of miners and industrial workers, against nuclear weapons, arms sales to repressive governments and the Falklands War. Won praise for pioneering work to fight poverty as government Minister for International Development.

- Winnie Ewing (born 1929): The first member of the Scottish National Party to be elected as an MP in the UK Parliament. Also a member of the European Parliament and of the Scottish Parliament.

- Margo MacDonald (1943–2014): Caring, passionate, witty Westminster and Scottish Parliament MP. Macdonald was a leading campaigner for Scottish independence. Supporters – and opponents – described her as 'a force of nature in Scottish life'.

Scotland should be grateful to them all.

"It is bitter slavery many have to endure in these factories..."

Mary Lennox, 1840

Lennox was a Chartist (campaigner for political reform, workers' rights and votes for working people) in a tough industrial district of Glasgow. Men called her 'a brazen-faced jade'.

"We wouldn't call the Queen our auntie..."

Scottish saying = 'we're as good as anyone'

CHAPTER THREE

WHAT ABOUT THE WORKERS?

Always, everywhere, in Scotland, women worked. And, from the earliest hunter-gatherers to later farmers and factory hands, from the grandest duchesses to the poorest cottagers, they were all proud of their skills. Their 'work' varied, of course, from gracious political hostessing to gruelling physical toil and all points in between. It usually involved, in addition, giving birth to children (dangerous and frightening – before around 1900, all mothers would have known other pregnant women who died) and being responsible for the whole household's food, domestic comfort and basic medical care.

Women did all this hampered by a legal system that for centuries put them almost entirely in the power of men, and by religion – old-style Catholic Christianity or new-style Protestantism – that regarded them as 'the weaker vessel', likely to sin themselves and to lead men astray.

Yet in spite of these very considerable disadvantages, Scottish women had a reputation as spirited and strong-minded. Unlike women in England, they did not change their names on marriage – a sign that they remained a member of the kinship group they were born to and did not 'disappear' into their husband's family. Were they all, as one fifteenth-century visitor to Scotland claimed, 'absolute mistresses of their houses and even their husbands…'? We don't know. It seems unlikely. However, to have survived and thrived, they must all have been hard-working and very, very capable.

We don't know the names of the earliest women workers – or indeed of most early working men. But we can catch glimpses of a few individuals in rent-rolls, tax lists and apprenticeship registers from medieval and early modern burghs (towns). Widows could own property; married women could trade independently from their husbands; girls could train at skilled crafts. We also see women named in records of alleged moral failings kept by the Kirk (Scottish Presbyterian Church) after 1560. The remains of women's material lives can be found throughout Scotland in surviving structures: prehistoric shell-middens and medieval shielings, black-houses, tenements, closes, wynds, tower-blocks and more. Also in the landscapes their hard work helped to create, as well as in museums.

Women mean business (1)

We know about these women because they all lived in Edinburgh, where records of their lives have been preserved. Similar working women doubtless lived in other Scottish towns.

- Janet Rynd (1504–1543): A widow, she traded in iron and also completed her late husband's charitable plans to build a hospital (refuge / nursing home).

- Janet Flockhart (died 1596), 'Wadwife' (moneylender): A widow with seven children, Janet inherited her late husband's merchant company and rented out lodgings. She used the profits to set up a very successful money-lending business. Clients included the Scottish Government. When she died, Janet's assets were worth almost £4 million at today's values.

- Mary Erskine (1629–1707): Shopkeeper and money-lender. Remembered today for generous gifts to build and maintain a boarding school, 'the Merchant Maiden Hospital', for the daughters of Edinburgh citizens.

Not only but also...

What women did at work depended on when and where they lived. In prehistoric times, 'work' might mean gathering shellfish, nuts and berries around the coast. From around 3000 BC, it meant growing crops and tending animals. And there were regional differences: in the Highlands, keeping livestock and hunting for wild food was more widespread than arable farming. Women and girls led cattle up to graze on high pastures in spring and summer, making and salting butter and cheese and living in rough shielings (huts). In the Lowlands, women weeded growing crops and, at harvest time, cut ripe grain with sickles, while men bound the stalks into sheaves and heaped them in 'stooks' to dry.

After the growth of Scottish towns (from around AD 1100) women increasingly became involved in trade: in their husbands' or fathers' workshops and counting houses (offices) or, as widows, running their own businesses. They also worked as food-processers and sellers: baking, brewing, dairying and managing market stalls.

At the same time, everywhere, women cooked, cleaned and spun wool which they took to local weavers to be made into rough cloth for their own use, or sold to travelling merchants. From around AD 1500, they earned cash by sewing, or by knitting small items of clothing.

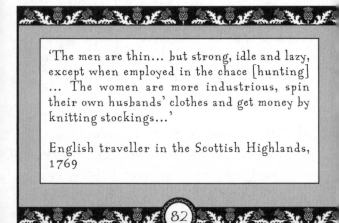

'The men are thin... but strong, idle and lazy, except when employed in the chace [hunting] ... The women are more industrious, spin their own husbands' clothes and get money by knitting stockings...'

English traveller in the Scottish Highlands, 1769

Multi-tasking

This extract from a ballad, 'Robin's Cure for a Bad Wife', lists just some of the household tasks that an ordinary famer's wife was expected to perform. It was published around 1810 by Thomas Johnstone of Falkirk, but the words are much older.

Robin's gone to the south country
refrain: Holland's green, holland
And there he's married a lady gay
refrain: Benty bows, Robin

The refrain is repeated between each pair of lines.

He's wed her and he's brought her hame
But well, I wat, she's a dainty dame

She winna wash and she winna wring
For wearing of her gay gold ring

She winna bake, she winna brew
For spoiling of her comely hew

She winna spin, she winna card [prepare wool for spinning]
But she will play her [flirt] with the Laird

Robin's come hame frae the plough
Cries 'Is my dinner ready now?'

You're a' mista'en Goodman says she
Do you think I'll Servant be to thee...?

The song does not end happily. Furious,
Robin kills a sheep and skins it, then ties the
sheepskin on his wife's back. 'I should not beat
my wife,' he says, 'but I can beat my sheep.' And
he does so. To avoid further violence, his wife
agrees to do all the domestic work he demands.

'Holland, green holland' is a typical street-cry
from a wandering cloth seller; 'benty bows'
means 'bow-legged'.

fishwives

Known as fishwives or fisher lassies, whatever their age and marital status, women living in coastal towns played a crucial part in Scotland's fishing industry. Strong, tough, no-nonsense and often bawdy, they faced bone-numbing cold and damp, skin sores caused by salt water, plus what today would be known as repetitive strain injuries. They had to endure the constant threat of bereavement, as well. Countless husbands, fathers, brothers and sons were lost at sea. As Scottish novelist Sir Walter Scott observed, about Scotland's fishing industry: 'It's not fish you're buying, but men's lives.'

Although, traditionally, it was bad luck for women (and black cats) to set foot on board a fishing vessel, fishwives worked extremely hard to complement men's efforts in many other ways. They dug worms and shellfish from shallow water for bait, fixed them – live and wriggling! – to fishing lines, tucked up their skirts and waded through the waves to carry fishermen on their backs to where boats were anchored, or else pushed the boats – with men on board – out into deep water so that they could sail away.

Fishwives gutted, filleted and packed fish in barrels. They smoked it and salted it to preserve it. They tramped miles with heavy creels (woven baskets that could weigh over 50 kg / 8 stone) on their backs to sell fish in their home ports or much further afield. Edinburgh fisher lassies, from Fisherrow, 8.5 km (5 miles) outside the city, were famous. The money they earned helped support their families, or was saved to buy new nets and even fishing boats.

Often, fisher lassies spent months away from home, sleeping in rough shelters, following the fishing fleet as it, in turn, followed shoals of herring migrating around the coast. Then, once railways were built across Scotland, they had to work extra-hard, against the clock, to gut, pack (ice and salt) and load the catch on to overnight trains, which hurried Scottish fish to markets in cities further south before it could spoil.

In the nineteenth century, after the invention of photography and the growth of tourism, fishwives became something of a tourist attraction. Women from Newhaven, in north-east Scotland, traditionally wore a striking costume of striped woollen skirts, shawls and kerchiefs. But it was not just this that attracted attention – it was because, as male writers noted at the time, fisherwomen were as strong and hardy as men. Their arms were brawny; their faces were tanned; some smoked tobacco. And they played male sports, as well: golf and football. In 1811, a golf club at Musselburgh, on the coast near Edinburgh, held a tournament for ladies. The prizes were silk handkerchiefs – and a new creel.

Christian Watt (1833–1923)

Born near Fraserburgh, on the north-east coast of Scotland, **Christian Watt** came from a fishing family. She began work aged eight, helping her fishwife mother, and married a fisherman.

Her adult life, first as a domestic servant, then as a fishwife and mother of ten children, was poor, tough and tragic. After her husband and two of their sons were lost at sea, Watt became mentally unwell, and was sent to an asylum. There, as therapy, she was encouraged to write her memoirs. She may have had help to do this, but the resulting text is a remarkable record of an extraordinary 'ordinary' life.

Slavery - in Scotland!

From 1606–1799, Scottish mineworkers – women and children, as well as men – were legally 'bondaged' to their employers, like slaves. They were not free to leave, and, if they did, they could be hunted down and forced to return to work.

'To the value of the property of 40 good colliers, with their wives and children, at the rate of £100 a-head…'

From a valuation of a colliery in Lanarkshire (west-central Scotland), 1771. The miners, together with the wives and children who worked alongside them, are valued like objects, as part of the stock in trade.

Scottish women miners did not dig coal. Their task was to climb up and down long, steep ladders, in the dark, carrying huge baskets of coal weighing up to 60 kg (9.5 stone) from deep inside the mine to the surface. Shifts were ten hours per day.

Mines and factories

Scotland pioneered the Industrial Revolution, for the rest of the United Kingdom and for the world. Mountains and lowlands of Scotland contained all the necessary materials: coal, iron and water. There were also thousands of Scottish people desperate to find work to pay for food and shelter. They had left poor, meagre farms and cottages in the Highlands and Lowlands – some were 'cleared' by landlords, but many chose to go – hoping for a better life elsewhere. Sadly, they did not always find it. They ended up labouring, sometimes in horrific conditions, in Scotland's new factories and mines, or as low-paid 'outdoor' workers in their own cramped homes.

'A living hell'?

Scotland's industrial cities grew very fast, and soon became overcrowded, dirty and disease-ridden. (In just sixty years, for example, the population of Glasgow increased from 250,000 to over 750,000.) Children born there faced a grim future. Like many other girls from poor families, **Mary Brooksbank** began work in a mill aged twelve; factory schools often held classes for mornings or afternoons only, so that children could work for the rest of the day. Working hours were long, wages were low – there were no UK laws to ensure equal pay for women until 1970 – and conditions in factories were dangerous. Clothes, fingers and long hair could get fatally entangled in machines. The other main source of work for young unmarried women was as domestic servants. That might also be physically tough, and servants were often poorly treated. They were kept busy for most of their waking hours, and had little personal freedom.

'The life of the women workers of Dundee right up to the thirties was ... a living hell of hard work and poverty. It was a common sight to see women, after a long ten-hour-day in the mill, running to the stream wash-houses with the family washing. They worked up to the last few days before having their bairns. Often they would call in at the calenders from their work and carry home bundles of sacks to sew. These were paid for at the rate of 5d for 25, 6d for a coarser type of sack.* Infant and maternal mortality in Dundee was the highest in the country.'

* Equivalent to about £1.15 in 2018.

Dundee jute-worker, Mary Brooksbank, *No Sae Lang Syne: A Tale of This City*, published 1968.

Industrial action

How to help? How to make things better? Working girls, wives and mothers joined together to improve their lives. Pioneer women trade unionists such as May Docherty, from a mining family in Fife, Dundee weaver Rachel Devine and Ayrshire book-keeper Mary MacArthur argued with women's employers to win better pay and working conditions, and arranged demonstrations by millworkers. In Dundee, women domestic servants set up a 'Maidservants Protection Association' and staged one of the first-ever strikes by working women, in 1872.

In Scottish industrial cities, women factory hands also campaigned for better working conditions, and fair pay. Some strikes were by women only, but usually female workers joined forces with men.

Red Clydeside – against injustice

Jane Rae (1872–1959) **The Singer Strike**
A needle-maker in the massive Singer sewing machine factory near Glasgow, Rae led 400 women to strike against restrictive new ways of working (harder tasks, less pay) imposed on them by company managers in 1910–1911. Within two days, most of the other 11,000 workers, men as well as women, had joined them. After threats from the company, the strikers reluctantly agreed to return to work. Rae and the 400 original strikers were sacked. Rae – always 'a fiery customer' – later became a left-wing political organiser and councillor, with particular interests in education and temperance. The example set by the Singer strikers, and by activists such as **Fanny Abbott** (1892–1971), also at Singers, encouraged many more Scottish industrial workers to join unions.

Mary Barbour (1875–1958) **'Mrs Barbour's Army'**
Carpet-factory worker and leader (with **Helen Crawfurd** and **Jean Ferguson**) of mass protests by thousands of working women

against steep rent rises in Glasgow and nearby towns in 1915. The 'Army' also held peaceful sit-ins and barred doors and windows to stop landlords evicting tenants – and chased away bailiffs trying to take household goods by threatening to pull their trousers down. As a result of Barbour's campaigns, new, fairer laws governing rent were introduced. Later, she became Glasgow's first Labour Party woman councillor. There, she called on the city to build public laundries, wash-houses and baths, children's playgrounds and welfare centres, and to give free milk to schoolchildren and pensions to mothers. She pioneered birth control services. She also became one of Glasgow's first women magistrates.

Helen Crawfurd (1877–1954) Women's Peace Campaign

Sunday school teacher and wife of a Church of Scotland minister, Helen Crawfurd was horrified by the poverty and squalor that working families in Glasgow had to endure:

'Human misery indescribable... appalling misery and poverty of the workers in Glasgow, physically broken down bodies, bowlegged, rickets... this appalled me and the drunkenness at that time was to me a horror.'

She defied the Church's view that a woman's main duty was to be a 'domestic angel' (home-based wife and mother,) and vowed to do all she could to improve poor women's lives. She campaigned for votes for women, to end the unjust treatment of prostitutes, and to improve women's pay and working conditions. She was chief organiser of the Women's Peace Campaign in Glasgow, which opposed the senseless slaughter of World War I. She joined Mary Barbour in leading women in the Glasgow rent strike.

After the war ended, Crawfurd was active internationally in radical left-wing politics, and supported demonstrators during the UK General Strike of 1926. She organised welfare services for poor workers from the Highlands of Scotland to the USSR, and became an outspoken campaigner against fascism in Europe.

Women mean business (2)

- Who put marmalade on the world's breakfast tables? Hard-working Scottish mother and daughter-in-law Janet (1736–1813) and Margaret Keiller (1800–1850). A story tells how Janet's husband John Keiller purchased a bargain cargo of oranges from a storm-bound Spanish ship. Instead of making them into jelly, Janet added little chips of peel. Hoots! Jings! Dundee marmalade! The story is picturesque but probably isn't true. Even so, Janet and Margaret did build up a successful business selling all kinds of jam and confectionery.

- What would you do? Tibbie Shiel (1783–1878) was left a widow with six children, and no money. So she turned her cottage near Ettrick in the Scottish Borders into an inn. The more guests the better; several in one bed at times! Tibbie's very crowded inn – and her character – became famous: celebrities came to see her. It's said that she still haunts the rooms today

- From famine to fashion. To help poor starving crofters after the potato famine of 1846–1847, landowner's wife Catherine Murray,

Lady Dunsmore (1814–1886), developed and promoted the traditional weaving industry on the Isle of Harris. Today, Harris Tweed is still made, and has become world famous.

- Gasping for a cup of tea? Need to sit down for a while? Go to a teashop – a new-style meeting place, with special rooms for women only. Teashops have been run in Glasgow since 1878 by eccentric businesswoman and art-collector Kate Cranston (1849–1934). The food is good. The atmosphere is refined. The artistic decorations are wonderful. And, most important of all for unaccompanied women, they are deeply respectable.

- Soup, glorious soup – and more marmalade. Ethel Baxter (1883–1963) married into a north-east Scottish family that ran a shop selling preserves. But Ethel had vision; she wanted the company to expand. She pioneered ways of canning and bottling local Scottish foods, especially the cleverly-named 'royal game' soup. Today, the Baxter company sells food products worldwide.

- The wheels on the bus… Ann Gloag (b 1942) founded international bus transport operation 'Stagecoach', with her ex-husband

and her brother. They famously used her father's redundancy payment to set up the company, then turned it into a multi-million pound business. Since retirement, Gloag has been involved in controversies, but has also given large sums to charity.

- Feel that your figure could do with a boost? You might like to try some glamorous new underwear sold by Glasgow entrepreneur and former model Michelle Mone (b 1971). They say she's brought special technology from the USA to create her designs.

' They seldom observe
any medium in their
passions, or set any
reasonable bounds to
those actions that result
from them. **'**

*Anti-Jacobite pamphlet, 'The Female Rebels' c 1745
quoted in Maggie Craig,* Damn' Rebel Bitches, *1997.*

CHAPTER FOUR

GALLUS BESOMS* – WOMEN WHO BROKE THE RULES

No, you couldn't trust them: Scottish women, that is. Or so said many Scottish men. Wilful, unreasonable, unreliable, immoderate, women needed to be kept under control, or who knew what might happen? As Robert Burns wrote, half in fun, whole in earnest, if the worst came to the very worst, women might even take over:

'If ye gi'e a woman a' her will
Gude faith! She'll soon o'er-gang ye...'*

*Gallus = bold, defiant, independent-minded; besom = stroppy or 'difficult' women.

*o'er-gang = overcome, overpower

Fortunately, for their own (and others') safety, sanity and satisfaction, Scottish women paid little attention to rubbish such as Burns's song. Few went quite so far in breaking the rules of 'decent', orderly female behaviour as, for instance, the Scottish suffragettes (see page 121), but many other Scots women did what they felt they should, regardless of social conventions or male expectations.

Some gallus Scottish women are well known. Robert Burns even named his horse (!!) after one of them: **Jenny Geddes** (c 1600–1660). A humble vegetable-seller in Edinburgh market, Jenny found herself in the spotlight at a time when passionate religious opinions were causing strife throughout Scotland. Way back in 1560, the new Protestant Church of Scotland had decided to get rid of old traditions and officials. Scots Church leaders and their congregations preferred a simpler, more democratic, way of worshipping. However, King Charles I (of Scotland and England) wanted to bring back the old ceremonies. Like many – maybe most – Scots, Jenny was not pleased. Perhaps for reasons of national pride; perhaps because of reluctance to change;

perhaps from religious conviction. Probably, a mixture of all three.

To earn some extra money, on Sundays Jenny worked as a 'waiting woman', going early in the morning to Edinburgh's St Giles Cathedral to bag a good seat for her employers, who did not arrive until the service was due to begin. One fine Sunday in July 1637, the Minister began to read from an old-style, written-in-England prayer book. Jenny lost her temper. She flung her folding stool at the astonished clergyman, and, if traditional tales are true, cried out:

'Diel gie you colic, the wame o' ye, fause theif; daur ye say Mass in my lug?'
[Devil rot your guts, you scoundrel! How dare you say Mass in my hearing!]

Jenny's protest led to riots, at first in Edinburgh and then throughout Scotland. The next year, thousands of Scots signed a National Covenant (document declaring support for the Protestant Church of Scotland and criticising King Charles). Many felt so strongly that they signed in blood.

Her story = our story

Jenny was just one of many Scottish women who rebelled against political authority, even if some of their stories are symbolic, rather than factual. For example, Scottish national traditions tell of **Marion Braidfute** (c 1276–1297), the wife or lover of William Wallace and mother of his daughter, and how she helped stiffen his resolve to fight against English invaders, and was later captured and raped by them. However, historians cannot find evidence that Wallace was ever married, or that Marion herself existed. More probably, she was invented, many years later, in a different political climate, by the Braidfute family, hoping to prove that they were descended from Scotland's national hero.

Fast forward a few centuries and there is, however, plenty of evidence to prove that **Lady Agnes Campbell** (1526–1601) was real, and that she really fought against the English. After Campbell's first Scottish husband died as a prisoner of war, she married Irish chieftain Turlough Luineach O'Neil in 1569. She brought with her a dowry of 1,200 Highland

soldiers, and personally took command of them in battle against the English who were fighting to take control of Ireland. Campbell was also a capable diplomat, speaking French and Latin as well as English and Gaelic. She led negotiations with English commanders to make sure that her husband, also a rebel, did not lose his vast estates. With **Finola O'Donnell**, her daughter, she encouraged Scots nobles to join the Irish in their fight.

'Damn' rebel bitches'

Even better-known rule-breakers are the Scottish women, from all different social classes, who supported the Jacobite claimants to rule Scotland (and England) from the 1680s to the 1740s. Most of them took no part in the fighting, contenting themselves with passing on secret messages or making and wearing garters and rosettes of white ribbon, to show their support for the cause.

Once the Jacobites were defeated, ribbons could easily be hidden. Life was less easy for women who played an active part in the rebellions. They were labelled 'bitches' –

disreputable and unclean. They were also accused, like so many other dissident females, of not being proper women:

'She is dressed in a semi-masculine riding habit of tartan trimmed with lace, with a blue bonnet on her head and pistols at her saddle…'

'Colonel Anne', Lady Anne Mackintosh

Lady Anne Mackintosh (1723–1784), described above by English enemies, was born into the staunchly-Jacobite Farquharson clan. She married, for love, it was said, an officer in the new Black Watch regiment that had been recruited to police the Scottish Highlands after the 1715 Jacobite rebellion. He held strong anti-Jacobite opinions.

When Bonnie Prince Charlie (see page 35) arrived in Scotland in 1745 to lead a new Jacobite uprising against the Hanoverian kings of Britain, 'Colonel' Anne hurried to support him, leading over 300 men from her husband's and father's lands. She used money – and a gun – to 'persuade' them to join her. Tipped off by her mother-in-law that a Hanoverian army was approaching, Anne sent a small group of her men out at night to shout, stamp, wave their plaids and clash their weapons – and scared the enemies away.

After this, Anne had the military, if not personal, satisfaction of seeing her husband captured. In a neat reversal of the usual practice, he was released into her safe-keeping. Later, in 1746, Anne helped Prince Charlie reach safety in the city of Inverness. But after the Jacobite army was crushingly defeated at the battle of Culloden, Anne herself was captured. Her high rank and personal charm protected her from severe punishment, and, after being left to cool her heels for a while, she was set free. Again, it is said that once the rebellion had ended, 'Colonel' Anne and her husband lived happily together, in spite of their political differences.

'Genteel… handsome… sprightly'

Searching for a deeply respectable rebel? Then clan leader's sister **Jean 'Jenny' Cameron** (born c 1700) might be just who you want.

Married but separated from her husband, Jenny kept house for her brother, acting as his companion and advisor. Lively, intelligent, brisk and 'agreeable', with sparkling eyes and jet-black hair, Jenny was one of the first women – or men – to join Bonnie Prince Charlie's rebellion in 1745. She went with her brother to greet the Prince when he landed.

Several stories tell how Jenny put on a tartan doublet (male waistcoat), picked up a sword, marched along with the Prince's army – and became his mistress. ('Immorality' was another accusation routinely hurled at women who disobeyed the rules.) However, almost certainly, the stories are not true. Like any practically-minded housekeeper, Jenny realised that money – or supplies – were far more useful to Prince Charlie than female companionship. So she gave him a herd of cattle – a very valuable present – and stayed peacefully at home, managing her brother's lands and caring for the local poor.

Not so lucky

As we have seen, some well-connected Jacobite women were pardoned. Others, like **Lady Margaret Ogilvy**, were sentenced to death – but she daringly escaped, disguised as an old servant, who she paid to take her place on the day of the execution.

Don't worry! The servant escaped, too, but other poor Jacobite women were not so lucky. For example, **Anne MacKay** from the Isle of Skye travelled to Inverness in search of her Jacobite husband, who was missing, presumed dead. While there, she helped two male Jacobite prisoners escape, by distracting the soldiers who were guarding them. As a punishment, the guards beat her cruelly and then forced her to stand for three days without food or water. She was left with a permanent disability, hardly able to walk for the rest of her life.

A cunning plan... or cherchez la femme...

Sometimes, women found that female 'unimportance' could be a positive advantage. No-one in authority expected them to be doing anything clever or remarkable, so no-one suspected them. By keeping calm and pretending to go about their daily lives as usual, women could break the rules, support the causes they believed in and not be discovered. Here are two – no, three – examples:

Grizel Hume, later Baillie (1665–1746) was only a child during the bloody Covenanters' wars that followed Jenny Geddes' protest (see page 102). But she was loyal, brave and daring enough to be trusted, aged twelve, with a dangerous secret mission. Her task was to carry a letter to an old family friend, Covenanter Robert Baillie. He had been thrown into gaol for fighting against King Charles, and was suspected of taking part in fresh plots against him. If Robert or Grizel had been caught, they would have been put to death as traitors. And in fact Robert was later executed, in 1684.

Helped by Baillie's young son, Grizel delivered the message. And then she risked another secret mission, after her father was also put in prison. This time, her task was to smuggle supplies, so that he would not starve. She hid the food under her apron; her father survived.

Once Grizel's father was freed, the whole family fled to France. They returned to Scotland in 1689, where Grizel was reunited with her childhood friend and helper, Baillie's son. After turning down several richer, grander suitors, yes, you've guessed! – she married him.

Further south, in the Scottish borders, admirers of **Midside Maggie** (Margaret Lylstone, born around 1630) told a similar story of female subterfuge. Maggie's husband was a farmer in wild, bleak countryside. Every year in June, he had to pay rent to the laird, a hard, brutal character. One year, after a bad winter, Maggie and her husband had no money. Maggie went to the laird to plead for more time, but he was unforgiving. 'Next year, I want two years' rent,' he said. 'Either that, or bring me a snowball on Midsummer Day! If you can't, I'll throw you off the farm.'

Maggie was scared; very, very scared. But then she had a bright idea. All winter, she collected snow, made it into a tight-packed ball, and hid it in the coldest, iciest place she knew, high up in the hills.

Midsummer came, and – yes – the snowball was still there. Maggie took it to the laird. He was impressed; they could stay on the farm, rent free, for ever.

Over the years, the farm did well but Maggie never forgot the laird or the snowball. One day, in 1651, she heard that the laird's enemies had put him in prison. So she took some flour, baked a bannock (like a cake), and hid gold coins inside it. Smiling sweetly, with eyes downcast, Maggie took the bannock to the prison. The laird found the money, bribed the prison guard – and was free!

Unsuspected

Would you – could you dare to do it? Ride on horseback close to the edge of windswept cliffs on the wild north-east coast of Scotland, ready to throw some of the oldest, most important and valuable Scottish treasures into the sea? **Christian Fletcher** (b c 1620) was the douce, obedient wife of a Church of Scotland minister. Yet that is what she did, in 1652. In law, it was stealing, and treason. She said she did it for Scotland.

Christian Fletcher was a royalist. At a time when Parliament in England was at war with Stuart kings Charles I and then Charles II, she supported the monarchs. Christian lived close to Dunnottar castle, in Aberdeenshire, and was friends with the Governor's wife. They were royalists, too – and guardians of the ancient Honours of Scotland: the crown, sword and precious jewelled items used when Scottish kings were being crowned. The Honours had been smuggled into the castle in sacks of wool by royalist women.

In 1651, Dunnottar was surrounded by Parliament's army. The siege lasted for months, but everyone knew that the castle could not hold out forever. They also knew that Parliament's soldiers would find, seize and destroy the Honours of Scotland. So how to save them?

Christian Fletcher volunteered. As a minister's wife, she was a pillar of the community. No-one would suspect her. So, together with a trusted maidservant, she hid the Honours (in a couple of pillows) and took them back to her husband's church, where they were buried for safety.

It was 9.5 km (6 miles) from the castle to the church. Christian took the most dangerous clifftop route, just in case she was being followed. Her plan? To throw the Honours down to the rocks below, to stop Parliament's soldiers grabbing them. But she knew, of course, that, if the soldiers caught her, they'd hurl her over the cliffs, too.

Alternative identities

Rebels, plotters, smugglers, protesters – they were all brave and daring. But what are we to make of women who refused to conform to society's norms for female behaviour in very different ways?

Let's meet 'scholar and gentleman' **Mary Diana Dods** (1790–1830), for example. Daughter of a grand, wealthy Scottish nobleman and his mistress, Dods was clever and well-educated (she spoke several languages) but penniless. To make money, she tried to run a school, but that failed and so she turned to writing. Using a male pen-name, 'David Lyndsay', she published books, stories and reviews with top Scottish publishers. All were much admired and Dods soon made friends in London's leading intellectual circles, including *Frankenstein* author Mary Shelley.

Fearing that her work would not be taken seriously, Dods kept her sex secret from publishers. That was not unusual for the time – or now. What was strange, however, was Dods's appearance; she cut her hair short like a man, and wore a male-style tight jacket and straight, narrow skirts that were more like wide trousers than feminine fashions.

Stranger still, and this time dressed in complete male attire, Dods 'married' an upper-class English girl who had disgraced her family by having a baby out of wedlock. The pair were probably not lovers; the 'marriage' was to save the unwed mother from further shame.

Using a different male name, 'Walter Sholto Douglas', Dods created yet another identity. With her 'newly-married wife', she went to live in France as an outwardly 'normal' couple, and tried to establish a whole new career as a diplomat. But she failed, and, aged forty, died of disease in a French debtors' prison.

The good doctor

Dods strayed beyond society's expectations because of personal preference, but also to earn a living and make good use of her skills and talents. The same was probably true of Scotland's most famous cross-dresser, **Margaret Ann Bulkley**, aka Dr James Barry (1789–1865), though recent research has suggested that he / she might also have had a rare combination of male and female physical characteristics. Whether that is true or not, Barry was raised as a female, yet steadfastly chose to live and work as a man.

At a time when women were banned from all higher education, Dublin-born Barry disguised him / herself, studied at Edinburgh University, qualified as a surgeon and had a very successful career in the British army that lasted for forty-six years. She / he won respect and admiration for organisational as well as surgical high standards, performing one of the first successful caesarean sections and ending his / her career as Inspector General of British army hospitals worldwide. Although slight and rather feminine looking, Barry was tough, brave and determined, not hesitating to reprimand even the formidable nursing pioneer Florence Nightingale.

A true original

However personally unusual, Dods and Barry both chose to follow respectable male careers: literature and medicine. But Dundee-born **Frances 'Fanny' Wright** (1795–1852) had no time for respectable occupations – and very little use for most other social conventions. Born soon after the French Revolution of 1789, and inspired by American colonists' bid to win freedom from British rule, Wright was a true original: bold, passionate, free-thinking, headstrong, dangerously impulsive and genuinely devoted to admirable ideals: truth, freedom and equality.

Wright was the daughter of a wealthy Dundee merchant with an interest in political reform. Both her parents died before she was three years old; she was left a large sum of money. She was brought up in England and returned to Scotland aged sixteen to continue her studies. In Glasgow, the sight of a shipload of dirt-poor Scottish migrants heading for a better (they hoped) life in America made Fanny think that 'something must be done'. She vowed to dedicate her life to putting right 'the grievous wrongs that seemed to prevail in society'.

In secret, aged twenty-three, Fanny sailed for the USA. There, she began a speaking tour, shocking her audiences with outspoken protests against marriage, big business and organised religion, and support for sexual freedom, legal rights for women and compulsory equal education. She was especially outspoken in her attacks on slavery, calling it a 'pestilence' and 'hateful'. She then went for a while to live in France, where she wrote books describing – and criticising – American society.

In 1824, Wright returned to America to continue her campaigns against slavery. The next year, she purchased a vast area of land close to Memphis, Tennessee, and tried to set up an ideal community there, where men and women, black and white people, would all live in harmony, equal and free. She purchased slaves from farmers and gave them their liberty. But faced by debts, scandals and prejudice, the community collapsed. Many of the ex-slaves moved to Haiti, in the Caribbean, and Fanny lost most of her money. She spent her last years living in New York, where she invented a new style of dress for women (knee-length dresses over bloomers) and campaigned for ever more radical social change, including birth control and divorce. Scotland – and the USA – had never known anyone like her.

'I have wedded the cause of human improvement, staked on it my fortunes, my reputation and my life.'

Fanny Wright's own words, carved on her tombstone in the USA in 1852.

If you think there are some gallus besoms missing...

'The gude cause'

Peaceful campaigns calling for women to have the right to vote on equal terms with men began in Scotland soon after 1860. Middle-class women held suffrage tea-parties to spread the word; women's suffrage societies were founded in Edinburgh from the 1870s; suffragists organised meetings, wrote letters and pamphlets, and lobbied candidates at national and local elections throughout Scotland. A petition calling for votes for women attracted many male as well as female signatures. Women campaigning for workers' rights also supported 'the gude cause'.

Queen Victoria, a famous lover of all things Scottish, was most definitely not amused. She complained that 'this mad, wicked folly of women's rights' made her 'furious'. But the suffragists' polite, persistent and patient campaigning attracted many thousands of supporters.

The pace of protests changed dramatically after 1906, when a branch of Mrs Pankhurst's militant Women's Social and Political Union (the 'suffragettes') was set up in Edinburgh. Like their sisters in England, Scottish suffragettes believed that it was time to take action. In 1909, hundreds of suffrage campaigners, young and old, marched through Edinburgh with banners demanding votes for women. They included nine-year-old **Bessie Watson**, perched precariously on a horse-drawn cart, proudly playing her bagpipes.

The Edinburgh march and many other protests were masterminded by capable organiser **'General' Flora Drummond** (1878–1949), who wore a military-style tunic and rode a horse, just like a male army officer. As she explained:

'We... are a society to make things intolerable, so that the average man and woman in the street will say, "For Heaven's sake give the women what they want, and let's have peace".'

Scottish suffragettes – there were probably around 100 activists – took whatever opportunities they could find to annoy and

embarrass the government. They smashed shop windows, poured acid into post-boxes, burned down a church, a stately home and a railway station, threw eggs at politicians, and threatened to bomb Edinburgh's beautiful botanic gardens. In 1908, they surrounded Member of Parliament Winston Churchill as he walked through the streets of Dundee, forcing him to take refuge in a shed.

At Stirling, **Ethel Moorhead** (1869–1955) vandalised the iconic Wallace monument. At Balmoral, close to Queen Victoria's Scottish home, **Lilias Mitchell** decorated the golf course with flags in the suffragette colours of green, white and violet. **Arabella Scott** set fire to Kelso racecourse; **Maude Edwards** slashed a portrait of the King; **Janet Arthur** tried to blow up the cottage where Scotland's national poet, Robert Burns, once lived.

The suffragettes' protests were violent, but they were careful not to do anything that might endanger the lives of others. Harm 'property not people' was their watchword. However, many Scottish suffragettes, like their sisters in England, bravely endured physical and mental injury to themselves in support of their ideals. **Marion Wallace Dunlop** (1864–1942) was the first Scottish woman to go on life-threatening hunger-strike in prison, setting an example that many other suffragettes followed. **Ethel Moorhead** (1869–1955) was the first Scottish woman to be force-fed: a dangerous and humiliating procedure that victims likened to rape or torture. Many women subjected to it feared they were going to die.

Although the suffragettes' brave protests won magnificent publicity, the hard and dangerous 'men's work' done by countless ordinary women during World War I probably did more to persuade the British Government to change the law. Women were given limited voting rights in 1918, and finally won the right to vote on equal terms with men in 1928.

Making a difference

Of course, Fanny Wright did not meet **Jackie Mackenzie** (1926–1998), but they might have had some fascinating conversations. Born to a conventional, wealthy Scottish family, Mackenzie worked as an actor, a prize-winning TV reporter and presenter, and then became one of the first-ever Scottish – British – campaigners for gay rights. Earning respect as a brave trailblazer, she fought for tolerance and against injustice of all kinds.

Wright might also have enjoyed talking with novelist and free-thinker **Naomi Mitchison** (1897–1999). From a grand, intellectual Scottish background – close relatives were politicians and world-famous scientists – Mitchison was a socialist, feminist, eccentric and mystic who dreamed of, and called for, a better life for everyone, everywhere. She lived according to her own rules, dressed in flowing robes, and called herself 'a witch'. Looking back in 1979, she wrote 'what was so strange and striking was the feeling we all had that if we tried hard enough, the millennium [a new and better world] would come into being.'

‘There's aye a muckle slippy stane at ilka bodie's door.**’**

'There's always a big slippery stone outside everyone's door.'*

*Traditional Scots proverb meaning 'There but for the grace of God go I.'

CHAPTER FIVE

SAINTS AND SINNERS

They don't make them like they used to, for good or ill. Although this is perhaps an extreme example, few Scottish women nowadays could match the saintly self-sacrifice shown by the nuns of Coldingham in the Scottish Borders. (Nor would we want them to, of course.) It was said that to preserve their holy chastity when threatened by Viking attackers around AD 800, the nuns hacked off their own lips and noses to make themselves utterly unattractive.

That tale says more about later generations' taste for salacious stories than about actual Scottish women. But Coldingham did have a real-life saint, **St Aebbe** (c 615–683), who won fame for her political and diplomatic skills and as a teacher.

Aebbe was the daughter and sister of pagan kings of the Angles, who at that time ruled Bernicia (north-east England / south-east Scotland). In wartime, she fled for safety to the Scottish far west, where she learned about Christianity. She worked to make peace between her royal relatives and powerful churchmen, persuaded at least one queen and many other people to share her new-found faith, and established a double monastery, for monks and nuns, at Coldingham. It became a place of refuge and retirement for pious royal women, and a centre for political entertaining. Monks from stricter monasteries were not pleased – but that was their problem.

It was said that Aebbe could control the tides that swirled around the steep rocky site of her monastery by the power of her prayers. The cliffs there are still known today as 'St Abbs Head'.

More saintly Scots

We know that Aebbe existed. But what about other Scottish female saints from long ago, such as St Bride, St Triduana, or St Teneu? Their stories have similarities with each other, and with Aebbe's – all were the daughters of important men; all involve notions of holy purity combined with blood or sacrifice; all are magical, and to most modern readers, very hard to believe as fact. But for long centuries, these saintly women were revered. They were also thought to be powerful, and to help their devotees to survive.

St Triduana (lived sometime between AD 300–700) was said to have been born in Greece and to have travelled to St Andrews in Scotland with holy man St Rule. Nectan, king of the Pictish people, was attracted by her beautiful eyes and fell in love with her. But Triduana wanted to remain a virgin, dedicated to the Christian God. So she tore out her eyes and sent them to Nectan, 'skewered on a twig'.

Triduana's tomb became a place of pilgrimage; it was said that she miraculously cured many cases of eye disease. Her fame spread as far as Orkney, where St Tredwell's (= Triduana's) chapel and the nearby loch were believed until as late as the eighteenth century to have healing powers.

St Teneu (lived around AD 450–550): A princess from the royal family in Gododdin (the area near Edinburgh), Teneu was raped by a visiting Welsh prince. When her father discovered her pregnancy, he ordered that she should be thrown to her death from a high hill called Traprain Law. Miraculously, Teneu survived, and so, in a further attempt on her life, she was pushed out to sea in a fragile coracle. She drifted ashore in Fife, and sought shelter with a Christian holy man. There, she gave birth to a son, Kentigern (also known as Mungo, 'dear one'). Welsh legends say that she eventually married a different Welsh prince, then retired to a nunnery.

Kentigern became a Christian missionary, and the patron saint of Glasgow. St Teneu is remembered there, too. Today, 'St Enoch's Square' in the city centre bears a corrupted form of her name.

Was Teneu 'Scotland's first recorded rape victim, battered woman and unmarried mother', as some writers have (sensationally) claimed? Or is her story, like Triduana's, a set of moral tales, designed to teach the importance of faith, hope and trust, and to offer a special kind of strength to women at a time when most of them had very little power?

Saint, goddess, druid...?

Today, **St Bride or St Brigid** (c AD 451–525) is well-known as one of the patron saints of Ireland. But her mother was from the Pictish people of Scotland, and early Scottish worshippers built many churches in her honour. There is also another, deeper connection. St Brigid shares the name (it comes from a word meaning 'mighty') of a pre-Christian fertility goddess worshiped in Scotland and Ireland. Rituals honouring St Brigid, that survived until the nineteenth century, probably date back to pre-Christian times. St Brigid's feast day was celebrated at the beginning of February, on the same day as Imbolc, the ancient Celtic Spring festival.

Well, then. Was St Bride / Brigid a Celtic goddess transformed into a Christian saint? Was she, as medieval monks and chroniclers said, the daughter of an Irish chieftain who happened to share the goddess's name? Was she invented by early Christian missionaries, to attract new converts? Or was she, as some Irish historians suggest, a female druid (or similar) who became a Christian and converted goddess-worship into reverence for the Christian God? All options are possible.

Whoever she was, according to tradition, Brigid had awesome powers. Even as a child, she was remarkably generous, doing all she could to help the poor. She became a nun, used magic to make the High King give her land, then founded a monastery at Kildare (Chapel of the Oak)* on the site of goddess Brigid's shrine.

Remarkably for a woman, St Brigid was given the same powers as a bishop (male church leader), and the authority to supervise all monasteries in Ireland. Her own monastery became a great centre of Christian art and

*Celtic gods and goddesses were worshipped in groves of oak trees.

learning; beautiful illustrated manuscripts were created there.

Brigid died – most appropriately – at the festival of Imbolc. During her life and after her death, many extraordinary miracles were attributed to her. She was said to:

- calm the wind and rain
- turn water into beer
- control fertility in women, sheep and cattle
- increase farm produce: milk, butter and bacon
- blight fruit trees or send double crops
- make water gush from the earth
- heal with drops of her blood.

A visit from the Biddy

For centuries, people in parts of Ireland and the western isles of Scotland made 'Brideog' (Biddy) dolls out of dried grass, and special-shaped crosses out of plaited reeds. Young girls carried these in procession from house to house on St Brigid's day. This was thought to bring prosperity and fertility for the coming year; it was bad luck not to be visited.

Prophets and Protestants

Honouring saints was abolished in Scotland 1560, when religious rebels broke away from the Roman Catholic Church and organised a new Protestant way of worshipping. Scots women could not be ministers in the new Church, but they were encouraged to develop their spiritual life through prayer and Bible study. From around 1600, they began to write down – and talk about – their innermost thoughts. Here are just a few examples.

Elizabeth Melville, Lady Culross (c 1578–1640), 'a faithfull, vertuous ladie', devoted her life to religion, frequently neglecting her home and family to hear preachers and attend church services. She exchanged letters on religious topics with leading Scots Protestant churchmen. She also composed religious songs, and an epic poem, *Ane Godlie Dreame*, that inspired English author John Bunyan to write his much more famous *Pilgrim's Progress*.

Mistress Rutherford (c 1600–1635) wrote the first-known spiritual autobiography by a Scottish woman. In it she describes overpowering doubts about her faith and her alarming fear of the Devil. Just occasionally, she also records feelings of religious ecstasy: 'I may say I tasted of the powers of the world to come [heaven or Heaven on Earth].'

Around the same time, in 1633, Edinburgh merchant's wife **Alice Sutcliffe** composed *Meditations of Mans Mortalitie*. Her outlook, shaped by her faith, was not a happy one:

'Thou shalt find this World to be a Casket of Sorrows and grievances, a Schoole of vanity, a laborinth of Errors, a dungeon of Darkness, and Market-place of Cousenages [deceivers], a way beset with Theeves, a ditch full of mud and a Sea continually tost and troubled with stormes and Tempests.'

In Aberdeen, **Lilias Skene** (c 1626–1697) became a member of the Society of Friends (Quakers), a radical, democratic Christian group that was persecuted by Church of Scotland authorities. When male Quakers were thrown in prison, Skene led Meetings for Worship, managed Quaker business affairs and did all she could to get the prisoners set free. She also helped set up a Quaker school and composed religious poetry.

'Of a surprising genius [= skill]'

Her friends were startled. Her family (members of the Edinburgh elite) was horrified. But in 1731, only just out of her teens, **May Drummond** (c 1710–1772) decided to leave home and become a travelling Quaker preacher. As we saw on page 135, Quakers, with their democratic, free-thinking approach to religion, were viewed with suspicion and alarm by many Scottish people.

Even worse, or so May's family said, was her decision to speak in public. At that time, it was shocking for a woman to speak out even in church, and completely outrageous for May to want to stand in the streets, preaching to anyone, rich or poor, who stopped to hear her.

But that is what May did, and she was good at it. Tall, handsome, well-educated and gifted with what we might now call emotional intelligence, she was a great communicator: her 'surprising genius' attracted crowds. Her dramatic preaching style proved especially popular with young people, in England as well as Scotland. She became a celebrity and was invited to London to meet the Queen.

Almost everyone agreed that May was sincere in her beliefs. However, they accused her of wanting too much fame and praise for herself. In 1764, she was asked by the Quakers to stop preaching in public, and her licence to work as a minister was withdrawn.

In the last years of her life, poor and exhausted, May (just about) made peace with her family. Friends supported her with gifts of food and money until she died.

'Clothed in the Sun'

May Drummond broke the rules for polite female behaviour. But **Elspeth Buchan** (1738–1791) went much, much further, claiming that she herself was a saint with special privileges from Heaven. Born to a poor family in north-east Scotland, Buchan worked as a cow-herd and married a potter. But they parted, and she set up home in Glasgow where she enjoyed listening to popular preachers. She became convinced that she was a prophet, and that she could fill people with the Holy Spirit simply by breathing on them.

By around 1748, Buchan had attracted a group of followers, who called her their spiritual mother and declared that she was the mystical 'Woman Clothed in the Sun' mentioned in the Bible, who would cause a 'war in Heaven' between good and evil. Understandably, this alarmed the Glasgow burgh leaders, who ordered Buchan and her 'Buchanites' to leave.

Claiming to be guided by the star that announced Jesus's birth, the Buchanites headed to Dumfriesshire, where they set up camps in the woods, to wait (so they said) for the end of the world. Buchan told them that they would never die, but would fly through the air to heaven, or to a new heavenly city on earth. She also told them that, as saints, they could do no wrong. Scandalous rumours soon spread – of idleness, wild sex, unruly women, communal property and much more – but Buchan went on preaching, singing hymns and encouraging her own weird ways of worshipping.

When Buchan died, her closest followers hid her body and pretended she was still alive. When the truth was finally revealed, her 'holy community' collapsed and the Buchanites drifted away.

The Wigtown martyrs

Women preachers were ridiculed and / or viewed with hostility. But other Scottish women with strongly-held beliefs faced death, especially during the 'killing time' of 1680–1685, when rival Scottish Protestants fought over who should govern religion: the King, or Scottish Church ministers?

Anyone who refused to swear loyalty to the King was condemned as a traitor. In one particularly shocking execution in 1685, two Covenanter women, Margaret MacLachlan, aged sixty-three, and Margaret Wilson, aged only eighteen, were dragged to the beach at Wigton at low tide, bound to wooden stakes hammered into the shore, then left to drown as the waves rolled in.

Saints for today

During the past 200 years, religion in Scotland has become a private matter, no longer entangled with political power struggles. Some women have followed traditional faiths; others have turned away from organised religion. But many have still behaved in remarkable ways that in the past might well have been called 'saintly'. We can't list them all, but here are just a few examples.

Mary Slessor (1848–1915) grew up in the slums of Dundee, and started work, aged eleven, in a jute factory. But at home, she read all she could; church teachers lent her books and she became fascinated by the story of Scottish explorer and medical missionary David Livingstone. In 1876, she left Scotland to spend the rest of her working life in West Africa.

Slessor was a devout Christian, but she did not preach or blame – though she did try to stop local customs that she thought were wrong. Instead, for almost forty years, she offered practical help: healthcare, social welfare and education. She learned African languages and lived simply in local houses. She became known as 'Mother of all the peoples'.

Elsie Inglis (1864–1917): Tough, austere, uncompromising, and a born leader, Inglis was one of the earliest Scottish women to qualify as a doctor. In Edinburgh, she lectured on women's illnesses and set up a women's hospital and a midwifery training centre. She campaigned for votes for women and equal education for female students, and supported many other liberal causes. When war broke out in 1914, Inglis trained volunteer nurses, and offered to work at the front line as a doctor. (British Army leaders told her to 'go home'.) But the troops clearly needed medical care, so Inglis organised and ran a network of hospitals staffed entirely by women, in France, Greece and eastern Europe. There, she and her nurses worked in appalling conditions to treat wounded soldiers, although she was by then gravely ill. She was awarded high honours in Europe; Winston Churchill (then a Scottish MP) said that she and the women who worked with her would 'shine forever in history'.

Jane Haining (1897–1944): The only Scottish person, male or female, to be honoured in Jerusalem as 'Righteous Amongst the Nations', Haining came from a Protestant family and her faith sustained her throughout her life. She trained first for clerical work, and then as a missionary. In 1932 she was sent to Hungary where she ran, very successfully, a home for orphaned and abandoned Jewish girls. She often faced hostility as anti-Semitic political opinions grew increasingly popular in Europe. When war was declared in 1939, Haining refused to leave 'her girls', although she was ordered home to Scotland for her own safety. She turned the care home into a refuge for many other Jewish people, and, when they, and the girls, were sent to a concentration camp in 1944, she insisted on going with them. She died a few months later.

Maggie Keswick Jencks (1941–1995): Born in China to a wealthy Scottish business family, Maggie became an international expert on the design of Chinese gardens. She married an architect and together they created a beautiful garden in Dumfries. All looked lovely, until, in her forties, Maggie was diagnosed with cancer. She was treated by doctors and with alternative medicines, but realised that cancer patients might also benefit from a different kind of care, to help them never 'to lose the joy of living in the fear of dying'. In the last years of her life, Maggie worked tirelessly to help set up a centre in Edinburgh, housed in a new and lovely building and gardens. Her vision was for it to provide practical and emotional support, a space for relaxed meetings or quiet reflection, or simply to serve as a caring and beautiful place to be. Today, there are 'Maggie's Centres' all around the world.

Saint in the making?

Venerable Margaret Sinclair (1900–1925): Edinburgh-born Sinclair came from a very poor family. Devoted to the Catholic faith, she worked in factories – demanding the right to hang religious pictures above the machines – and then joined a strict order of nuns. After working with outcast people in London, she caught a disease, and died aged twenty-six.

Since Margaret's death, there have been calls to make her a saint. Pope John Paul II (no less!) declared that Margaret was ordinary but exceptional: 'one of God's little ones, who through her very simplicity, was touched by God with the strength of real holiness of life'. In 2017, a Glasgow priest claimed that he had been saved from death by praying to Margaret to help him.

Scandalous Scots

It's quite a step to turn from these saintly Scots to their much less admirable sisters. But the more we look at some of Scotland's most famous female criminals, the more we wonder just how wicked some of them really were.

Crimes of passion!

Understandable or unforgivable? There must have been countless 'domestics' during past centuries in Scotland, most of them unrecorded. But a couple of crimes, because they involved high-born women, have lingered in the public memory.

Jean Livingston, Lady Waristoun (1579–1600) was married to an older man from a rich and powerful family. He went abroad, leaving her pregnant. However, if we are to believe the traditional ballad version of her tale, when he came home and found her with a bouncing baby boy, he immediately doubted that the child was his, in spite of Jean's protestations:

'Now hold your tongue, my lady gay,
Nae mair falsehoods ye'll tell to me;
This bonny bairn is not mine,
You've loved another while I was on sea.'
In discontent then hame she went,
And aye the tear did blin' her e'e;
Says, 'Of this wretch I'll be revenged,
For these harsh words he's said to me.'

And revenged she was. After seeking advice from her trusty old nursemaid, Jean decided that her husband must die. She asked one of her father's manservants to strangle Lord Waristoun.

The crime – and Jean's part in it – were soon discovered. Just three days later, she was beheaded by a new arrival in Scotland, the 'Maiden' (guillotine). Her father did not try to stop the execution, but did arrange for it to take place at 4 am, to try to avoid bad publicity for his family. The nurse and manservant were also executed, very, very horribly.

Around eighty years later, the crime of **Christian Nimmo** (d 1679) was to fall in love – and lose her temper. Unhappily married, she sought comfort in the company of her charming neighbour (and relative) Sir George Forrester. For years, they carried on a secret love affair. Mistress Christian longed to leave her husband and marry Sir George. But he refused, saying the scandal would ruin him.

The lovers continued to meet, but one day Sir George did not appear at their usual rendezvous, a dovecot in the grounds of his home, Corstorphine Castle. So Mistress Christian sent a servant to find him. When he finally appeared, he was drunk and angry. They quarrelled; she reproached him; he called her a 'whoor'. Furious, she grabbed his sword, and stabbed him.

At her trial, Mistress Christian claimed that the stabbing had been an accident; she had hit out at Sir George in self-defence. This may have been true, but she was still found guilty, and executed.

Today, her ghost – the White Lady – is said to haunt the grounds of Corstorphine castle, carrying a sword still dripping with blood.

Body Snatcher...

William Burke and his partner-in-crime William Hare were notorious murderers. They killed at least sixteen – maybe more – victims in one year (1828), then sold the dead bodies to Edinburgh's medical schools for dissection. However, **Margaret 'Lucky' Log** (born c 1788), who married William Hare, has almost vanished from history. But, quite possibly, she was the mastermind behind the body-snatching; the murderous spree was her idea.

Like Burke and Hare, Log was a tough labourer who worked digging Scotland's new canals. When her job came to an end, she moved to Edinburgh and, to make a living, took in lodgers. Even before she met and married Hare, she might perhaps have 'disposed' of some of her visitors. She encouraged Hare, and soon after, Burke, his friend, to lure vulnerable people from the streets with offers of hospitality, and then to suffocate them.

When their crimes were discovered, Log and Hare gave evidence for the prosecution, and escaped punishment. Together, they fled to start a new life in Australia.

Baby farmer?

Was **Jessie Kean** (also known as Jessie King, 1861–1889) dreadfully wicked, or just a victim of Scottish cities' disease-ridden and insanitary living conditions? Born to a poor working family in Glasgow, Jessie moved to Edinburgh, married, and, in 1887, had a child. The baby died, just a few weeks old.

Perhaps Jessie longed for another? Perhaps she needed money? Perhaps she wanted to help poor working mothers by providing childcare? Or perhaps she was that terrible thing, a baby-farmer: someone who took in babies that other women did not want or could not care for, and made sure (for a fee) that the little ones were never heard of again.

Whatever the truth, Jessie was arrested after at least three babies she was 'caring for' died, one after the other. Yes, babies often did die in accidents or from disease, but the fact that one tiny body was found dumped on waste ground looked extremely suspicious. Jessie Kean was hanged as a murderer.

Poisoner?

It was a trial that fascinated newspaper readers all round the world. Did she do it? Did young, pretty **Madeline Smith** (1835–1928), cherished daughter of a rich and respectable Glasgow architect, really kill the man who said he loved her? The verdict (thanks to top defence lawyers hired by Madeline's father) was the Scottish sitting-on-the-fence 'Not Proven'. But if Madeleine didn't kill handsome clerk Emile L'Angelier, then who did?

The story is simple. Aged around twenty, Madeline met L'Angelier and seems to have fallen in love with him. They exchanged hundreds of passionate, and, for the time, daringly explicit letters. In some, Madeline calls L'Angelier her 'husband'. But he was poor, and Madeline's parents forbade a marriage. Instead, they encouraged her to get engaged to a young man with good prospects, and Madeline agreed. To avoid any future scandal, she asked L'Angelier to return her love-letters. He refused, and threatened to show them to her father, instead. Was he hurt and upset? Or was this blackmail, for money?

A few weeks later, Madeline purchased some arsenic – widely used at that time to kill rats, mice and flies. A few weeks later still, L'Angelier fell ill, saying he thought he had been poisoned – adding that if Madeline had done it, he would forgive her. Was this murder? Or was it suicide plus a bid to get revenge on Madeline for jilting her? Readers, you decide.

fraudster?

'Hellish Nell!' What a nickname! But from childhood, as well as being boisterous, **Helen Duncan** (1897–1956) claimed to be able to foretell the future. As a young woman, her life was gruelling: many children, not much money and exhausting work in Dundee jute mills. To earn more, and because she enjoyed the attention, Helen began to hold seances, at first just for friends and then for larger audiences.

In the years after World War I, spiritualism was popular, as bereaved families desperately tried to make contact with lost loved ones.

Helen claimed to receive messages from the dead, and also to produce 'ectoplasm' – a ghostly-white substance from the 'other side'. (In fact, it was fine knitted cotton.) Repeatedly arrested and fined for fraud, Helen was forced to stop her activities in 1941 after government intelligence agents accused her of giving away official secrets. She had been trying to 'materialise' a drowned sailor from a warship sunk by enemies. After a spell in prison, she resumed her seances as soon as the war ended. The police remained suspicious until she died.

Spy!

What's your image of a female spy? Mysterious, exotic, glamorous, seductive, and discreet and efficient, too…? Well, **Jessie Jordan** (1887–1954), a real-life spy who sent secrets to Hitler's Germany, was a plump and homely wee ladies' hairdresser in a run-down district of Dundee, and also rather careless … Born in Perth, Jessie married a young German waiter in 1912. They lived in Germany until he died. Later, she married again, but parted from her husband and returned to Scotland in 1937. Around the same time, a German 'friend' asked her to check some facts about Britain for him, and to forward any letters for him that arrived at her shop. Did Jessie know what she was doing? Yes, she did, though it's been suggested that she was blackmailed or otherwise forced into obeying her German handler.

An inquisitive worker at the salon soon began to wonder where all the letters came from, and called the police. Jessie was arrested and put in prison; after the war ended in 1945, she was sent to Germany where she died.

Yet more villains – or victims?

Today, few would consider these women criminals. But they suffered, all the same. So did many others like them, sad to say.

Half-Hangit Maggie (Margaret Dixon, died 1761): It's an old, old story. After parting from her husband, young Margaret Dixon found work as a servant at an inn. The innkeeper's son took a fancy to her; fearing to lose her job, Maggie gave in, became pregnant and hid her condition. The baby was born in secret, but it was weak and sickly. A few days later, it died.

Maggie took the body to the nearest big river, hoping that the waters would carry it away. But it was discovered. In 1721, Maggie was accused, convicted and hanged. Very sad. End of story?

No! Like other criminals, Maggie was cut down from the gallows and bundled into a cheap coffin. As this jolted through the streets on a cart, in the famously bracing Edinburgh air, 'half-hangit' Maggie began to gasp, and breathe, and came back to life again.

Lawyers said this proved that Maggie was not guilty. She was pardoned, reconciled with her husband, and lived for another forty years.

Shameless – guiltless?

The case of **Mistress Jean Weir** (c 1610– 1670) is even more troubling. One fine day, this Edinburgh spinster walked out into the streets, tried to rip off her clothes and said she wished to die 'with as much shame as possible'. Why? She was a secret worshipper of the 'Fairy Queen' and had sold her soul to the Devil!

Until then, Mistress Weir had led a quiet, respectable life. She and her brother were members of a zealous Protestant group, the Bowhead Saints, who gathered at their house for prayer meetings. What was going on?

Today, we would probably wonder about dementia, or say that the Saints' stern teachings had made Mistress Weir excessively anxious, or that lurid stories about the Devil had unbalanced her over-active imagination. But people in the past thought otherwise. Mistress Weir was executed, as a 'punishment' for her non-existent crimes.

'Wild beauty'?

Mad, bad or horribly abused? It's a tragic tale. **Rachel Chiesley, Lady Grange** (d 1745) came from a violent family. (Her father shot and killed a judge who dared to convict him.)

Famous for her 'wild beauty', Rachel attracted a noble husband and bore him nine children. But the marriage was not happy, and over the years her behaviour became increasingly strange. She disrupted church services, swore in the streets, and did all she could to bring shame upon her husband. She often talked about killing herself and slept with a sharp blade under her pillow.

From her husband's point of view, the final straw came when Lady Grange accused him of being a Jacobite (see page 34). He risked losing his lands, his money – and his life. In 1732, he arranged for her to be kidnapped. He told family and friends that she was dead, and held a funeral service for her.

In fact, Lady Grange had been carried off to a remote Scottish island, where she lived in a stone hut thatched with grass. After several years, she managed to send a message to her lawyer. But the rescue ship arrived too late. Her captors smuggled her away to a new hiding place and she died still a prisoner.

Which witch?

They weren't saints, but they didn't deserve to die. In Scotland many more witches were reported, and many more were executed, than in all other parts of the British Isles.

Most people, for much of the past, believed in some kind of supernatural power. Their ideas were shaped by organised religion, but often included notions from unofficial belief systems: charms, curses, healing spells and shamanistic contact with a 'spirit world' of demons or fairies. There were also rituals and superstitions designed to protect children, animals, farm crops, seafarers and more.

For centuries in Scotland, these old ideas were mostly ignored by people in power. But between around 1560 and 1700, they were labelled as 'witchcraft'. Anyone who appeared to believe in them was seen as a dangerous threat: to religion, the community and the state. At the same time, an accusation of witchcraft became a convenient way of silencing – or killing – awkward, unwanted members of the community or political enemies.

Historians have suggested many reasons for the 'witch-craze', ranging from intellectual fashions (a German book about witch-hunting became popular throughout Europe) to new Protestant beliefs, new ideas about government, new ideas about women and simple economic hardship.

A new law passed in Scotland in 1563 made witchcraft punishable by death. It was not repealed until 1723. Precise figures are not known, but around 5,000 people may have been accused during that time, and over 1,500 executed. Three-quarters of them were women. Here are just a few.

Margaret Burges (1579–1629): From Edinburgh, Burges seems to have been unpleasantly quarrelsome, and a bully. She cursed and threatened her neighbours and business contacts. They called her a witch and claimed she caused them actual harm. A young female servant also alleged that Margaret abused her. Verdict? Guilty!

Isabel Gowdie (lived around 1662): Remembered today for her answers to questions from hostile investigators, probably given after days and nights of sleep deprivation and repeated 'prickings' (stabbings with a long needle). Gowdie 'confessed' to dancing and drinking with other witches, meeting with the Devil, flying through the air and trying to use magic to do harm. But she also claimed to have visited fairy-land (in hollow hills, as described in Celtic traditions) and seen elves making fairy weapons. (Tiny prehistoric arrowheads could be found on local land.) Her confessions may reveal the 'thought-world' of uneducated women, in which ancient magic beliefs and folk customs mingled with Christian teachings.

Janet Horne (died 1727): The last witch to be executed in Scotland – and the UK – Janet was old, feeble and suffering from dementia. Her daughter had a disability: her hands and feet were differently formed. People said that Janet had used witchcraft to turn her daughter into a pony, so that she could ride to market, but had failed to return her to human shape. The daughter escaped punishment, but Janet was burned alive.

Grissel Jaffrey (died 1669): The last woman to be executed as a witch in Dundee; we know very little about her. But a local legend shows how afraid people were of being accused of witchcraft. It was said that her son, skipper of a merchant ship, was nearing harbour after a long voyage. But when he saw smoke and flames rising and learned the reason why, he headed back out to sea – and was never seen again.

Beatrice Leslie (1577–1661): A midwife, who used magic rituals to try to help mothers, but cursed people she quarrelled with. Along with six other women, she was tortured; this led to her 'confessing' that she had met the Devil in disguise. She was strangled and burned.

Euphame MacCalzean (c 1558–1591): Said to be bossy and strong-minded, and from a rich, powerful family, she also had connections with enemies of King James VI. MacCalzean was alleged to have used witchcraft to ease the pains of childbirth and to try to kill her husband, whom she did not like. With other 'witches' at North Berwick, she was also accused of raising storms that would sink ships. MacCalzean was burned alive – and King James VI used the story of the North Berwick witches to terrorise his enemies.

Agnes Sampson (died 1591): One of the North Berwick witches. A traditional healer, she used incantations based on Christian prayers. She claimed these would cure – and cause – diseases. This angered and alarmed Church leaders; she was tortured and confessed to other, invented 'witchcraft' crimes.

Woman witchfinder!?

At the height of the witch-craze, local judges paid spies to ride out on patrol, searching for suspicious behaviour. Most Scottish witchfinders were men, but one, Christian Caldwell (lived 1660s), was a woman in disguise. She dressed in men's clothes and called herself John Dicksone. We don't know how many 'witches' she caught, if any. But later, she was accused of false accusations and torture, and of causing the deaths of innocent victims.

Words about women

Robert Burns describes a witch dancing, in his poem Tam o' Shanter (1791):

'There was ae winsome wench and waulie,
That night enlisted in the core,
Lang after ken'd on Carrick shore;
(For mony a beast to dead she shot,
And perish'd mony a bonie boat,
And shook baith meikle corn and bear,
And kept the country-side in fear.)
Her cutty-sark, o' Paisley harn
That while a lassie she had worn,
In longitude tho' sorely scanty,
It was her best, and she was vauntie...'

(There was one lively, attractive young woman / Taking part in the coven that night / Later, she was famous in the Carrick district / She killed many cattle / Wrecked many fine ships / And ruined lots of oats and barley / The whole countryside was afraid of her. She wore an underskirt / of fine cloth made in Paisley / She'd had it since she was a girl / It was very, very short / But it was her best, and she was proud of it...)

❝If you are given two options, take the harder one because you'll regret it if you don't...❞

*Scottish-based climber **Alison Hargreaves** (1962–1995), the first woman to reach the summit of Mount Everest without help from Sherpas or supplies of oxygen.*

See page 166

CHAPTER SIX

TO BOLDLY GO – SCOTTISH WOMEN PIONEERS

I f later, unreliable reports are to be believed, weak and sickly **Isabella Bird** (1831–1904), sent on a sea-voyage by her doctor, threw her tight corsets overboard and became a new woman, full of energy and zest for adventure. If that story is not true, then it ought to be. Once far away from polite, 'cramped' (as Bird called it) Edinburgh society and its restrictions, she found the freedom to be the woman she wanted to be.

That woman was a traveller and adventurer. Bird was born in England but moved to Edinburgh when young. However, she spent a large part of her life away from home, exploring the landscape and encountering different peoples in America, Australia, Hawaii, Japan, China, Indonesia and the Middle East. The books she wrote about her travels became very popular: she was the first woman to be made a fellow of the elite Royal Geographical Society.

Back in Scotland, Bird loved to travel to the Western Isles. Shocked at the poverty of the people living there, she gave money from the sale of her books to help crofters emigrate to a new life in America.

Unrecorded

Bird was remarkable, and well-known. But of course, women have been pioneering for hundreds of thousands of years. If they had not observed, reflected, made plans and dared to try something new and life-changing, humanity would not have survived. Who else, in the past, fed babies, raised children, nursed invalids, cared for homes and shelters, made clothing, and grew, stored and cooked food? However, the names of these early women practical pioneers are not recorded.

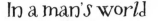
In a man's world

The past 250 years have also seen a very different type of pioneer: a woman who has won success in a male-dominated field, such as business, sport, the Church or the professions. Thanks to their courage, energy and determination, the old legal and social barriers are – slowly – breaking down.

Changing hearts and minds – and laws – has never been easy. And pioneering women have often had to make difficult choices. Work or children? Campaigning or career? Personal ambition or partnership with compromise? Public protest or private persuasion?

Law-abiding behaviour or something publicity-seeking and possibly illegal? Way back in 1913, Scottish suffragette **Lila Clunas** (1876–1968) encouraged pioneering women to stay true to their ideals, however fierce the opposition. For the sake of the future:

'In this country in the past men have defied the laws, and today their names are revered.'

follow your dream

Just three months after completing 'one of the greatest climbs in history' (see page 162), Alison Hargreaves died in a freak storm on another Himalayan mountain, K2. She was only thirty-three, and left two young children. Several years later, her husband explained why he did not try to stop her pioneering:

'I loved Alison because she wanted to climb the highest peaks her skills would allow her to. That was who she was…'

Interview in *The Guardian*, 2002

To the frozen North...

Isabella Bird's travels took her all around the globe, but Scottish Polar explorer **Isobel Hutchison** (1889–1982) concentrated her studies on just one region. A keen botanist and pioneer film-maker, she documented the Arctic natural environment and the everyday lives of peoples in Iceland, Greenland and Alaska. Her films and paintings created a valuable record of fast-changing societies.

Another Arctic adventurer, **Myrtle Simpson** (b 1930), is usually remembered today as 'the mother of Scottish skiing'. President of the Scottish Ski Club, she was also the first woman to ski across Greenland unsupported, and only the tenth woman (in over 150 years) to be awarded the prestigious Polar Medal.

...and tropical Australia

Countless Scottish women pioneered new settlements in Canada, Australia, South Africa and New Zealand. Few, however, were as controversial as traveller and castaway **Eliza Fraser** (c 1798–1858).

Fraser sailed from Orkney with her sea-captain husband in 1835. They landed in Australia and then steered north. But their ship hit a coral reef and sank. The survivors clambered into boats and headed back to Australia. Some died along the way; others came ashore and met Aboriginal people, who were understandably suspicious. Fraser's husband and several crewmen were killed, but she survived. However, she later complained that she was made to work like a slave by Aborigine women. Today, historians think that Fraser may have misunderstood the Aboriginal way of life.

Fraser was found by search parties, and returned to European settlements in Australia. Sadly, she – and newspapers who interviewed her – tried to profit from her experiences, telling lurid stories, portraying Aborigines as 'savages' and asking for money from the public. Was Fraser 'artful' and 'wicked', as some who met her claimed? Or traumatised and confused after her shipwreck ordeal?

Medical matters

In 1870, a mob led by male medical students at Edinburgh University jeered and threw mud at a group of seven young women attempting to enter an examination hall. Soon afterwards, the men chased a frightened sheep around the room. It was chaos; the exam was abandoned.

Why all the fuss? The male students, backed by many male academics and large numbers of the public, were trying to stop **Sophia Jex-Blake** (1840–1912) and other members of 'the Edinburgh Seven'* from taking an exam in anatomy – an essential part of their course to train as doctors.

Already, the previous year, 1869, the 'Seven' had caused outrage. They were the first-ever women allowed to study at a British university. But Edinburgh's male doctors, teachers and students did not want them. They feared women would be a distraction in class and a threat to the male-only medical profession. The Edinburgh public thought that women

* Sophia Jex-Blake; Isabel Thorne; Edith Pechey; Matilda Chaplin; Helen Evans; Mary Anderson; Emily Bovell.

examining bodies, as students or doctors, would be disgusting.

But Jex-Blake was not the woman to avoid an argument. Forceful, hot-tempered and tactless, she was determined to be a doctor. She left Edinburgh to study in Switzerland, qualifying in 1877. At the same time, and just as important, she worked with other female campaigners to set up the London School of Medicine for Women (1874), and with a sympathetic male Member of Parliament to get the law changed to allow all British universities to admit female medical students.

In the 1880s, Jex-Blake returned to Edinburgh to work for the rest of her career as a doctor and teacher of midwifery. She founded another new hospital there, for women and children, and another college to train female medical students.

Trailblazer **Gertrude Herzfeld** (1890–1981) became the first woman surgeon to practise in Scotland, in 1914. A less confrontational character than Jex-Blake, she showed what intelligence and quiet determination could achieve. She won respect from male colleagues for her operating skills, and for her teaching, publications and research. As well as working at Scotland's top hospitals, she was medical advisor to charities and institutions caring for many people with disabilities.

Nurse, nurse!

Around the same time as the Edinburgh Seven were trying to study to be doctors, yet another formidable personality, **Rebecca Strong** (1843–1944), was transforming nursing in Scotland. One of the first pupils trained by legendary Florence Nightingale, Strong was also said to have been the first nurse allowed to take temperatures using technology: a mercury thermometer! Appointed matron of the biggest hospitals in Dundee (in 1873) and then Glasgow (1897), she worked tirelessly to improve nurse training and nursing care. Her innovations ranged from new, hygienic nurse uniforms to lectures on the latest surgical techniques, and her training system was soon copied worldwide. She also tried to improve the care offered to nurses themselves, campaigning for decent living accommodation for hospital staff, and setting up clubs where off-duty nurses could find support and friendship and share new ideas.

Marriage according to Marie

A pioneer in two very different fields – fossil plants and family planning – Edinburgh-born **Marie Stopes** (1880–1958) lived a life full of controversy. She studied botany in London, Germany and Japan, and was the first woman lecturer appointed by Manchester University in 1904. Like other feminists of her age (and since) she argued for greater equality between marriage partners: 'Too often, marriage puts an end to women's intellectual life.'

Marie's own unfulfilled marriage also led her to study the biology of human reproduction. In 1918, she published *Married Love*, a book that shocked readers in Britain and worldwide. It was soon followed by another: *Wise Parenthood*. Both contained explicit advice on birth control. Stopes believed that having smaller families would ease the burden on poor parents, and give educated women the chance to continue their careers. In 1921, she opened Britain's first family planning clinic for women. Although facing strong opposition, from doctors and lawyers as well as organised religion, Stokes continued to speak out for the rest of her life.

Jeanie, Jeanie full of hopes
Read a book by Marie Stopes
But to judge from her condition
She must have read the wrong edition!

Children's rhyme, quoted in Ruth Hall, *Passionate Crusader: The Life of Marie Stopes*, Harcourt, Brace, Jovanovich, 1977 page 5.

Taking action

In Scotland and elsewhere, many women followed the example of these bold pioneers, doing their best, in their own individual ways, to fight injustice and improve people's lives. Here are just a few examples.

Ethel MacDonald (1909–1960): Anarchist campaigner; volunteer on the Republican side during the 1930s Spanish Civil War. Made pioneer broadcasts from Spain to England about the plight of captives and refugees; risked her life to help hundreds escape persecution.

Rachel Buchanan (1915–2008): Pioneered local services for people with mental disabilities and their families, at first in her home town, and then across Scotland.

Maidie Hunt (1916–1977): Pioneer of women's leadership in the Church of Scotland and international religious organisations. Campaigner for equality, international development and world peace.

Ruth Adler (1944–1994): Philosopher, who helped improve justice for children, prisoners and women. Also worked for Amnesty International (human rights charity), and helped set up Scottish Women's Aid.

Lorna Young (1952–1996): Pioneer of the Fair Trade movement in Scotland; campaigner for international development.

Remzije Sherifi: Radio journalist forced to flee from Kosova during the 1990s Balkans War. Found asylum in Glasgow; used her own experiences to help run services for other refugees and migrants. Nominated as one of Scotland's Women of the Year, 2017.

Roza Salih (b 1989) and **Amal Azzudin** (b 1990): Two founders of the 'Glasgow Girls': young women from diverse backgrounds in a deprived area of Glasgow who campaigned for better treatment for asylum seekers. They won support from Members of the Scottish Parliament, and the Scottish Government agreed to change immigration rules.

Independent-minded

Wendy Wood (1892–1981) Artist, writer, eccentric, campaigner. In 1928, she was one of the founders of the National Party of Scotland (now SNP). In 1932, she tore down the Union flag from Stirling Castle and replaced it with one showing a Scottish lion. In the 1950s she led campaigns against Elizabeth II signs on Scottish post-boxes (they were removed). In the 1960s she tried (and failed) to get the Church of Scotland to back the SNP independence campaign. In 1972 she went on hunger strike to call for Scottish independence.

Kay Matheson (1928–2013): The only woman among four students who removed Scotland's Stone of Destiny from Westminster Abbey, London, in 1950. Their bold act – technically, it was treason – won 'breakthrough' publicity for the SNP.

Women of God

Lady Grisell Baillie (1822–1891) was named after her famous ancestor (see page 110). The two shared a strong Protestant faith, and the second Lady Grisell devoted a large amount of her time and money to the Church and to charity. She believed that women's contribution to Church life should be encouraged and recognised. She became the first-ever deaconess (spiritual helper and welfare worker) within the Church of Scotland in 1888.

Vera Kenmure (1904–1973) is usually said to be the first woman minister in an 'official' Scottish Church, in 1928. A supporter of many women's causes, Kenmure liked to begin her prayers, 'O Father, Mother, God'. However…

In 1912, American **Olive Winchester** (1879–1947), the first woman graduate in divinity at Glasgow University, was made minister of a small Protestant group in Glasgow. She returned to America in 1914.

Boats and cars and planes...

Traditionally, women were not welcome as skippers or crew on sailing ships, although wives did sometimes accompany high-ranking husbands as passengers. Unusually, Dundee-born **Mary Buick** (1777–1854) smuggled herself on board the navy warship where her husband had been forced to work. She ended up nursing wounded sailors and helped to pickle the dead body of war-hero Admiral Lord Nelson in brandy, to preserve it.

Around 1830, **Betsy Miller** (1792–1864), from Saltcoats on the River Clyde, was faced with a difficult decision. Her brother had just drowned at sea and her father was old and ill. Debts were mounting; the family shipping business faced ruin. What should she do? Although no longer young, Betsy took command of her brother's ship, and set sail. It was a terrible risk, but Betsy learned fast. She became a skilful sailor: the first woman ever to be certified as a ship's captain by the UK Board of Trade.

As well as storms and dangers at sea, and hard,

dirty work with machinery, pioneer marine engineer **Victoria Drummond** (1894–1978) also had to face prejudice and hostility from the men she sailed with. Yet she achieved a series of brilliant 'firsts': Britain's first qualified female marine engineer, first woman Merchant Navy chief engineer, first woman to win a Board of Trade Certificate as a ship's engineer, and first woman offered membership of the professional Institute of Marine Engineers. During World War II, after her ship was bombed, Drummond also won awards for outstanding bravery. Alone, in great danger, she kept the engines running!

Dorothée Pullinger (1894–1986) trained as an engineer at a time when women were not welcome in heavy industry. But aged twenty, during World War I, she was appointed 'Lady Superintendent' of an armaments factory employing thousands of women. In 1919, she helped set up the Women's Engineering Society, to encourage and support female engineers. In 1920, she helped create the 'Galloway', the first (and only) car specially designed for women, and supervised its production in a Scottish factory run by women.

From childhood, **Winifred Joyce Drinkwater** (1913–1996) was fascinated by flying. It was daring, exciting – and very, very new. In 1930, aged seventeen, she became Scotland's youngest trained and licensed pilot. Two years later, she became the first Scottish woman to gain a commercial pilot's licence. Making regular flights over Scotland, her work included delivering newspapers to remote islands, air-sea searches for shipwrecked sailors, air-ambulance services – and aerial surveys to help hunt for the Loch Ness Monster.

...and bikes...

Already keen motor-bike riders – before 1914, they competed in motorcyle and sidecar trials – Highland-born **Mairi Chisholm** (1896–1981) and her friend **Elsie Knocker** (1884–1978) volunteered as despatch riders for the Women's Emergency Corps during World War I. Braving danger, and surrounded by terrible suffering, they ferried wounded soldiers and dead bodies from the front line to army hospitals, on bikes and in early saloon cars converted into ambulances. In 1915, they set up and raised all the funds for their own dressing station, just 90 m (100 yards) from the trenches, to provide rapid emergency treatment. Their daring won them fame and many awards for courage.

After the war, Chisholm went back to racing, but in cars, not motorcycles. Much later, in the 1950s, two dashing (in all senses of the word) Scottish sisters, **Annie** (1924–2004) and **Christina Neil** (1927–1991), became some of the first women drivers to compete in the gruelling Le Mans Rally.

...and a bus driver!

Little is known about her life, but in 1940, **Helen 'Ellen' Armstrong** passed the test to drive a single-decker public service vehicle (first time, with flying colours). She is the first-known Scottish woman who qualified to drive a bus; her sister, Susie, soon followed her example. A whole generation later, Glasgow-born **Karen Harrison** (1960–2011) became the first woman in Britain to work as a train driver, confronting, and surviving, what she called 'this gigantic tidal wave of hate' from railwaymen.

Legal ladies

- Chrystal Macmillan (1872–1937): Scientist, suffragist, lawyer and campaigner for women's education. One of the founders of Women's International League for Peace and Freedom; delegate to international peace negotiations after World War I.

- Margaret Howie Strang Hall: In 1900, applied to take the exams that would qualify her to practise law in Scotland. (She pointed out that the rules described exam applicants as 'persons', without reference to sex or gender.) Permission was refused by the highest court in Scotland.

- Madge Anderson (1896–1982): The first professional woman lawyer in the UK. Became a Scottish solicitor in 1920, just one year after rules were changed to allow women to practise law.

- Dame Margaret Kidd (1900–1989): First female Scottish advocate (barrister); the first woman King's Counsel (senior lawyer) in Britain.

- Lady (Hazel) Cosgrove (b 1946): Advocate; Queen's Counsel; first woman Senator of the College of Justice (= judge in Scotland's Supreme Courts).

- Baroness Helena Kennedy (b 1950): Leading barrister; worked to win equal opportunities for women in the legal profession. Expert in human rights law, civil liberties and constitutional issues.

- Lady (Leeona) Dorrian (b 1957): Advocate. In 2016, the first woman to be Lord Justice Clerk, the second most senior judge in Scotland. The highest-ranking woman ever in Scotland's legal history.

- Dame Elish Angiolini (b 1960): First woman Solicitor General for Scotland, then first woman Lord Advocate (head of Scottish government law services). Worked to improve legal services for children, minority groups and crime victims. 'There is still a great deal to be done to ensure that... prosecutors defend the rights of the weakest and the worst amongst us.'

The strange case of Stout Marjory

Dundee mill-worker **Marjory Panton** (lived 1890s) took just one small step towards fair treatment for women, but a pioneering one.

In 1892, Panton tripped at work and injured her ankle. She stayed at home for eight days, to recover; when she returned to the mill, her (male) manager questioned her about her health, saying that she was 'uncommonly stout'. Then, in front of the other workers, he asked her to get her doctor to write to him, confirming that she was not pregnant.

Panton was outraged (and so was her doctor). At that time, to be pregnant out of wedlock was a deep disgrace, not only for the woman concerned but for her whole family. Panton asked for an apology; the manager refused. Panton sent a solicitor's letter, asking for compensation for the damage to her good name. The manager refused again, so Panton took him to court. After a long legal struggle, and attempts by the factory management to trick Panton into withdrawing her complaint, she was paid a large sum, and the case was settled.

'A fair cop'

Yes, that honestly was the title of a TV programme celebrating the appointment of the first female police officer in Britain (in England, in 1915). Scotland had to wait a few years longer until the first Scottish, uniformed policewoman was sworn in: **Jean Thomson**, in Dundee. Before then, however, Glasgow had employed **Emily Miller** as the first 'lady assistant' to male police in Scotland. Miller's job description was changed to 'policewoman' in 1919, but she was not given equal powers with male officers to arrest suspects until 1924.

If paid police work was 'a man's job', volunteering was a different matter. Glasgow and other cities recruited women as special constables, for example 'Big Rachel'. Said to be over 2 m (6 ft) tall and weighing 108 kg (17 stone), her task was to control rioters.

The world around us

From one of the very few women to have a potato named after her, to one of the world's first 'greens', Scottish women have pioneered developments in farming, environment and heritage.

We know little about **Elyza Fraser** (1734–1814), except that she took a keen and untypical interest, for her time, in new farming methods. Male admirers reported: 'This lady is a miracle for farming. Her genius (intelligence, skill) must be uncommon, to exceed so eminently in a vocation that nature seems to have confined to the male sex.'

One of the first Scottish women to train as a professional gardener, in 1912, **Madge Elder** (1893–1985) worked for great estates before setting up her own plant nursery business. Her knowledge and taste won admiration for her garden designs. Long before other gardeners became media personalities, she wrote regularly about plants for popular Scottish newspapers and magazines.

Lady Eve Balfour (1898–1990) began and ended her life with pioneering ventures. In 1915, she was one of the very first women to study agriculture at university. In 1919, she began to run her own farm and became increasingly interested in new ideas about sustainable agriculture, setting up large, long-term experiments to compare traditional and organic farming methods. Convinced that organic was better and healthier, in 1943 she presented her ideas in a book, *The Living Soil*. It became a classic. In 1946, she was one of the founders of the Soil Association, which still encourages organic farming worldwide. The 'Lady Balfour' variety of potato, which grows well in organic conditions, was named in her honour.

Beautiful, eccentric and outspoken, actress **Marjorie Linklater** (1909–1997) became a pioneer 'green' campaigner, when her beloved North Highlands were threatened by the dumping of nuclear waste. Passionate about the countryside and its natural and historic heritage, she also played a leading role in preserving and encouraging the cultural life of Orkney, especially music and art.

For around twenty years (1905–1925), pioneer photographer **M E M Donaldson** (1876–1958) trekked through wild countryside, dragging a heavy camera to take pictures of people and places. Her photos created an amazing record of vanishing West Highland life.

Today cookery is fashionable, and so writer and historian **F Marian McNeill** (1885–1973) is remembered for her book *The Scots Kitchen* (1929), one of the very first to celebrate Scottish ingredients and traditional recipes. But McNeill also worked to collect and record Scottish folklore and language, and played a leading part in the early years of the Scottish Nationalist movement.

Historian and researcher **Elsie Grant** (1887–1983) was also fascinated by the ordinary lives of Scots in the past. She travelled widely in the Highlands, interviewing older people and collecting traditional items from cottages and farms. Inspired by Scandinavian folk-life museums, Grant opened Scotland's first museum of Highland life in 1944. Her work preserved a huge amount of information and objects that would otherwise have been lost.

Sporty Scots

All winners. All remarkable. All pioneers...

Helen Matthews 'Mrs Graham' (b 1857): Pioneer of women's football. Led a female team to tour Scotland; played the first-ever football international (against England) in Edinburgh in 1881.

Belle Moore (1894–1975): Swimmer. Youngest Scottish – and British – woman to win Olympic Gold (aged seventeen).

Marjorie Langmuir (1905–1984): The first woman – there has only ever been one other – to represent Scotland at international level in three sports. She played hockey, tennis and badminton.

Ellen King (1909–1994): Swimmer. Six British swimming championships, two world records, and two silver medals in the 1928 Olympics.

Jessie Valentine (1915–2006): Golfer. Won the British Women's Amateur tournament four times and was ranked as world's number one female golfer. 'The Scot who has done the most for the game.'

Nancy Riach (1927–1947): 'One of the greatest swimmers of her generation.' By the age of eighteen she held twenty-eight British and Scottish records; tragically caught polio, collapsed during a race and died aged only twenty.

Helen Elliot Hamilton (1927–2013): Table tennis World Champion.

Elenor Gordon (1933–2014): Swimmer. The first Scottish woman to win gold at the Commonwealth Games. Pioneered the new butterfly swimming stroke.

Winifred Shaw (1947–1992): Tennis player (doubles). The only Scot before Andy or Jamie Murray to have reached a Grand Slam final.

Isabel Newstead (1955–2007): Paralympic athlete. Won ten gold medals (and many others) in three events: swimming, javelin and shooting.

Rose Reilly (b 1955): 'Best UK female football player of all time.' Played for French and Italian clubs,* where she was a top goal scorer. She captained the Italian national team in the 1983 Women's World Cup – and scored the winning goal.

Judy Murray (b 1959): Tennis player. Won many Scottish titles. Coach to her sons Jamie and Andy Murray, and many other players. For a while captain of UK Federation Cup (women's) team. Campaigns to promote sport and fitness for women and children, and in deprived areas.

Liz McColgan (b 1964): Distance runner. Gold medal World Championships; also medallist at Commonwealth Games and Olympics. Set new Scottish records for half-marathon and 10,000 metres.

Margaret McEleny (b 1965): Swimmer, Paralympics. World and European record-breaker.

---

* *Women were banned from playing football professionally in the UK until 1971.*

Shirley McIntosh (b 1965): Shooting. First Scottish woman shooter to win Olympic Gold.

Rhona Martin (b 1966): Curling. Won gold at the 2002 Winter Olympics; coach of the Scottish national team.

Shirley Robertson (1968): Sailing. Won gold at two Olympics.

Dame Katherine Grainger (b 1975): Rowing. 'In a class of her own.' Has won more medals than any British female athlete, ever, at four consecutive Olympic games. Also works in sports leadership, and for charity.

Eve Muirhead (b 1990): Curler. Olympic medallist; youngest-ever skipper of a World Championship winning team, 2013.

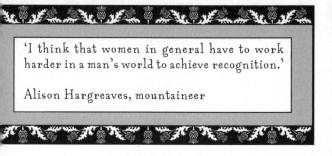

'I think that women in general have to work harder in a man's world to achieve recognition.'

Alison Hargreaves, mountaineer

‘ Like a man's, only weaker and poorer... **’**

Art by women, described by
Dr William Fettes Douglas,
Director of Glasgow School of Art, 1885

‘ You make me want to SHOUT! **’**

Song, performed (very loudly) by
Scottish singer Lulu (now known
as Lulu Kennedy-Cairns), 1964

See page 203

CHAPTER SEVEN

PURE DEAD BRILLIANT!*

Hindsight's a wonderful thing. In 1826, a young Scottish woman, **Jane Welsh Carlyle** (1801–1866), wrote to a friend, complaining about her husband: 'He thinks we [women] are an inferior order of beings.' In his lifetime, Jane's husband, Thomas Carlyle, became an international literary celebrity, and Jane was known chiefly as his unhappy wife. But today, Jane is remembered and admired as a formidable 'forgotten talent'; the hundreds – thousands? – of candid, clever letters that she wrote take us right to the heart of nineteenth-century life.

* *Scottish saying meaning 'Exceptional; the best'.*

Seeing stars

Jane Carlyle was – is – just one among so many creative Scottish women: writers, artists, musicians, actors, scholars and teachers, past and present. Who to choose as examples? Readers, that's not easy! Especially since they all excel in very different ways. Let's begin with the scholars. What would Jane's grumpy husband have thought of them?

The world's first scientist

It's a pretty cool sign of respect to have a new word invented in your honour, but that's what they did for Scottish mathematician **Mary Fairfax Somerville** (1780–1872). In 1834, the word 'scientist' was coined to describe her remarkable ability to understand the latest, most advanced mathematical and scientific ideas and to explain them clearly to others.

Gentle and charming (she was nicknamed 'the Rose of Jedburgh', her home town), Somerville was nonetheless a determined and independent-minded child. Although told to limit herself to feminine occupations such as sewing, she had a passion for reading the scholarly books in her father's library, and loved to observe nature and collect shells, fossils and plants. Her brother's tutor let her borrow mathematics textbooks; Somerville was fascinated.

As was expected of young women, Somerville married. Her husband disapproved of female education, but he died young, leaving Somerville with enough money to live as she chose. And she chose to study – the most difficult and important astronomy and mathematics of her time. Her second husband, a doctor, encouraged her; together they moved to London where Somerville tutored another great female mathematician: young computer pioneer Ada Lovelace.

Moving again, to Italy, Somerville translated, edited and added her own ideas to works by Europe's top mathematicians and astronomers, making their discoveries comprehensible to scholars, students and teachers worldwide. She also wrote about physics, chemistry, botany, geography, geology and a new area of study, microscopy. In 1835, she became the first woman member of the elite Royal Astronomical Society, with Caroline Herschel.

Towards the end of her life, in spite of all her achievements, Somerville regretted that she had not concentrated on her first love, mathematics. Then, she said, she might have written 'something more useful'(!) Today, an asteroid, a crater on the moon, a river in the Arctic and the first women's college at Oxford University are all named after her.

'The Queen of Science' (The Times, London, 1872)

'...[She] has done more to remove the light estimation in which the capacity of women is too often held than all that has been accomplished by the whole Sisterhood of Poetical Damsels and novel-writing authors.'

Scottish poet Joanna Baillie, about Mary Somerville.

Housemaid - superstar!

Another Scottish astronomer, **Williamina Fleming** (1857–1911) is remembered today for inventing a new system for describing phenomena in the night sky, and for cataloguing an astounding 10,331 different stars. Leaving Scotland with her husband, Fleming was abandoned in America and found work as a maid in the home of a university astronomer. He noticed how intelligent she was, and offered her a job as a 'human computer', measuring and recording the position, colour and brightness of stars. Fleming became an expert in analysing telescope images of the night sky, making many exciting discoveries such as wonderful 'white dwarfs'. She was the first woman to manage teams of astronomical observers and to be in charge of a university's astronomy photo archives.

The stuff of life

In Edinburgh, **Charlotte Auerbach** (1899–1994) pioneered another new and exciting area of scientific study: genetics. Born in Germany, she studied biology and chemistry but fled to Scotland in 1933 to escape anti-Semitic persecution – and began a brilliant career. In 1942, she was one of a team of three who showed how chemicals could cause mutations (changes in genes) in living cells. Their discovery had an enormous impact on the study of life-sciences, and on the diagnosis and treatment of many diseases.

And there are more...

- Elizabeth Blackwell (1707–1758): Unusually for a woman, Blackwell compiled and published a scientific book under her own name. It was a 'herbal': descriptions of medicinal plants with her own wonderful illustrations. It was used by doctors and nurses for many years.

- Elizabeth Fulhame (lived c 1790): Pioneer chemist, who experimented to discover the properties of metals. She also found out that light acting on metal compounds created permanent pictures – one of the first steps towards photography.

- Dame Maria Gordon (1864–1939): Geologist who investigated movements of the Earth's crust to discover how mountains had been formed.

- Muriel Robertson (1883–1973): Studied tropical parasites and the bacteria that infect wounds. Her researches helped doctors understand and find cures for killer diseases.

- Isabella Gordon (1901–1988): Marine biologist; expert on sea-spiders and crabs. The first woman to be appointed to the full-time staff of the British Museum. Honoured by fellow biologist Emperor Hirohito of Japan.

- Marion Gray (1902–1979): Studied maths in Edinburgh and the USA. While working as an engineer for an American telecoms company, she discovered a new kind of graph, still used by mathematicians today. It was given her name.

- Marion Ross (1903–1994): Researcher in nuclear and X-ray physics and later in fluid dynamics (movements). One of the very few women to work for the British Admiralty during World War II, on underwater acoustics (sound) and hydrodynamics (movement of fluids).

Fast forward to today, there are brilliant Scottish women working in pure research and applied science. Here are just two of the most famous.

Professor Karen Vousden (b 1957): Cancer researcher, for years based at the famous Beatson Institute in Glasgow; in 2018 appointed Chief Scientist to Cancer Research UK. After studying genetics and microbiology, Vousden worked to investigate molecules involved in preventing the growth of tumours, opening up new possibilities for life-saving treatments.

Professor Dame Sue Black (b 1961): One of the world's leading forensic pathologists, Professor Black has inspired respect for the compassion and humanity of her approach to what must be at times a frightful and sickening task. She has won honours for her work in identifying the remains of victims in the Balkans and other civil wars, and in the human chaos that resulted from the Indian Ocean tsunami of 2004.

Education, education, education...

Yes... there were, and are, world-class Scottish scholars, but hundreds of thousands of educated women made their contribution to Scotland's future by working as schoolteachers. The ideas of sisters **Rachel** (1859–1917) and **Margaret Macmillan** (1860–1931) were revolutionary in their lifetimes and are still followed today. They pioneered adventure play and outdoor activities for children and campaigned for school meals and school health services.

Airs and graces

Turning to the worlds of music and drama, we have more Scottish stars to choose from. It's hard to imagine what Jane Carlyle's husband might make of pop princess **Lulu** (b 1948), suddenly-famous 'I dreamed a dream' **Susan Boyle** (b 1961) or uber-cool singer and campaigner **Annie Lennox** (b 1954). And how would he rate singer-songwriter **Emeli Sandé** (b 1987), Brit-Award winner **Eddi Reader** (b 1959) and folk-rock performer **K T Tunstall** (b 1975)?

Violinist **Nicola Benedetti** (b 1987) – also a pioneer of inclusive music education – and brilliant percussionist **Dame Evelyn Glennie** (b 1965) are clearly in a class of their own, but let's not forget Scottish women composers, **Thea Musgrave** (born 1928), **Judith Weir** (first female Master of the Queen's Music, b 1954) and **Sally Beamish** (b 1956). Would Mr Carlyle think they were inferior, too?

Born just a few years after Jane Carlyle died, Scottish soprano **Mary Garden** (1874–1967) certainly did not consider herself 'inferior'. Applauded from Paris to Chicago, she was one of the first operatic leading ladies who could act as well as sing. Top composers (Debussy, even!) wrote especially for her. Garden's feuds with rival singers – and her tempestuous love-life – were also legendary.

Back home on the Isle of Skye, housemaid and wool-worker **Mairi MacPherson**, known as Big Mary of the Songs (c 1821–1898), composed poems and songs in Gaelic that were praised for their energy and spirit. They were not always friendly, however. One verse begins 'How I hate the English speakers …'.

Also in Gaelic, Mull island crofter **Mary MacDonald** (1789–1872) wrote the words for a new Christmas carol ('Child in the Manger') and set them to a Highland tune now named 'Bunessan', after her home village. Today, that tune – with alternative words, 'Morning has broken' – is well-known worldwide.

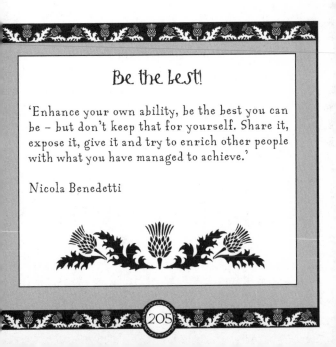

Be the best!

'Enhance your own ability, be the best you can be – but don't keep that for yourself. Share it, expose it, give it and try to enrich other people with what you have managed to achieve.'

Nicola Benedetti

Land o' the Leal

From a different social background, **Carolina Oliphant** (Lady Nairne, 1766–1845) composed songs and poems celebrating Scottish history, beliefs and traditions. Although seen today as over-sentimental, they were extremely popular in their time.

I'm wearin' awa', John
Like snaw-wreaths in thaw, John,
I'm wearin' awa'
To the land o' the leal.
There's nae sorrow there, John,
There's neither cauld nor care, John,
The day is aye fair
In the land o' the leal.

Carolina Oliphant

awa' = away; snaw = snow; aye = always; leal = faithful

This is verse 1. Later verses tell how the singer, who is dying, looks forward to being reunited with her dead child, and then her husband after he dies, in the Land of the Leal.

Still in the world of the performing arts, **Harriet Siddons** (1783–1844), the daughter, wife, sister and daughter-in-law of well-known actors, had a long and impressive career. When young, she sang and performed in works by Shakespeare and other classical authors; after her husband died, she took over management of the leading theatre in Edinburgh, where she staged newly-fashionable plays with Scottish themes.

Much less classy – though they sound amazing – Italian actresses and acrobats **Signora Violante** (c 1682–1741) and her daughters also made their home in Edinburgh. Famous for daring 'rope dances', they also ran a dancing school for young ladies.

From Aberdeen, and yet another theatrical family, **Jessie Fraser** (1801–1875) wowed audiences as a young woman; fans wrote her poems and deluged her with flowers. After marrying another actor, Fraser and her husband pioneered touring theatre companies that braved harsh conditions in northern Scotland to perform popular plays.

More recently, fragile blonde **Mary Ure** (1933–1975) won awards for creating roles in new and daring British dramas on stage and in film. Glamorous redhead **Moira Shearer** (1926–2006) began her career as a ballet dancer, but shot to stardom in her first major film, *The Red Shoes* (1948). Scottish beauty **Deborah Kerr** (1921–2007), cool, poised heroine of *The King and I* (1956) and many other Hollywood dramas, was awarded an honorary Oscar for a lifetime of achievement.

Today's Scottish female screen stars include **Kelly MacDonald** (b 1976; *Trainspotting*), **Karen Gillan** (b 1987; *Dr Who*) and **Katie Leung** (b 1987; *Harry Potter*). There is also, of course, the inimitable comedy talent of **Elaine C Smith** (b 1958), and the strange, ethereal beauty of actor and performance artist **Tilda Swinton** (b 1960). On the other side of the camera, the work of Scottish 'film-poet' **Margaret Tait** (1918–1999) was overlooked for most of her life, but is at long last being recognised for its pioneering vision.

Aye, write!

When it comes to literature, it's even more difficult to select examples – there is so much female Scottish skill to choose from. Although, as (male) Scottish novelist Irvine Welsh points out:

'The establishment, the newspapers, they try to create something called Scottish literature, but when people are actually going to write... they'll write what they feel.'

Take **Joanna Baillie** (1762–1851), for instance. Slow to read and write – she called herself 'dull' – Baillie was enchanted by the first play she saw performed, at school, and grew up to become one of Scotland's most celebrated dramatists. Her plays were heroic and romantic; many were set in Scotland.

A wild and noble Scottish chieftain! A handsome seducer! A brave heroine who escapes across Canada, alone, in a canoe! **Mary Brunton** (1778–1818) was devoutly, dutifully religious, and wrote novels with a purpose, to guide and to warn. (The first had the forbidding title, *Self-Control*.) But modern readers might say that Brunton's imagination betrayed her. They remember her exciting plots, rather than the moral message.

Susan Ferrier (1782–1854) was another devout writer, but, even so, her stories were fun. Sometimes compared to Jane Austen, her novels mock foolish people and customs in Scottish society, and express her admiration for clever, capable Scottish women.

Baillie, Brunton and Ferrier were all part of Edinburgh's urban, educated elite. Ferrier also knew the West Highlands. But **Nan Shepherd** (1893–1981) lived in the northeast of Scotland and her novels, poems and pioneering books about the landscape are all set there. She is most famous today for *The Living Mountain* (1977), 'the finest book ever written on nature and landscape in Britain'. Unlike mountaineering books by men, it is not about quest or achievement. Instead, it is a meditation about the Cairngorm Mountains and what they can mean. Shepherd is one of the very few women anywhere to be pictured on a national bank-note: a Scottish £5.

A mixed bunch. As Scottish poet **Liz Lochhead** (b 1947) wrote: 'Ah dinna ken whit like your Scotland is.' Of course, Lochhead is herself one of Scotland's brightest stars, and was Makar (Scotland's national writer) from 2011–2016. Her works, mostly in Scots, often start with a simple idea and then take the reader on a powerful emotional journey. Like Robert Burns, no less, she can say something profound in words a child could understand.

The honour of being Scotland's Makar has passed to novelist **Jackie Kay** (b 1961). Her works explore issues of identity; Kay is female and gay and of part-African heritage. Her writing has been called 'subtle… graceful.. haunting... dreamlike'.

As a further example of Scotswomen's literary prowess, the UK's royal Poet Laureate is also Scottish. **Dame Carol Ann Duffy** (b 1955) uses sharp wit, accessible language and startling originality to search for truths about lives and experiences. As she herself says, 'I like to use simple words, but in a complicated way.'

Not only, but also...

So many good writers, not enough time to read all their books!

- Janice Galloway (b 1955): Novelist, broadcaster; works with composers to write words for music.

- Val McDermid (b 1955): Novelist; crime-writer. Some of her 'tartan noir' books explore violent and disturbing topics.

- Ali Smith (b 1962): Novelist, short story writer, academic. 'One of the most inventive novelists writing in Britain today.'

- Aminatta Forna (b 1964): Novelist, memoir-writer, professor of creative writing. Her works look at how we perceive and explain.

- A L Kennedy (b 1965): Novelist, journalist, broadcaster, stand-up comic. Her work is dark, dryly witty, full of insight.

- Louise Welsh (b 1965): Novelist and short story writer. Her books are questioning, challenging, sometimes terrifying.

The 'creme de la creme'*

- Dame Muriel Spark (1918–2006): One of *The Times*'s top ten writers since 1945, Spark's works have been described as 'slim as stiletto blades – and as deadly.'* Outwardly light and witty, they tackle troubling topics: the nature of good and evil; the abuse of power. Readers, this is heresy, but I find them mostly too cruel, or maybe too truthful, to enjoy.

and again:

- J K Rowling (born 1965): You either love the *Harry Potter* books or you loathe them, but you can't deny that adopted-Scot Joanne Rowling has done an awful lot of good, for children's reading and for charity. With almost 500 million copies sold, *Harry Potter* has persuaded a whole generation of reluctant readers – worldwide – to see the point of books, and that is a very considerable achievement.

---

* *Clever schoolgirls, as described by Miss Jean Brodie, heroine of Spark's novel* The Prime of Miss Jean Brodie.
* The Guardian, *2018*

The 'Spook School'

Thank goodness, not all men dismissed women's creative work as second-rate. Indeed Charles Rennie Mackintosh, probably Scotland's best known artist / architect, considered his wife's work better than his own: 'Margaret has genius; I only have talent.' Textile artist, painter and designer **Margaret MacDonald** (1864–1933) and her sister **Frances** (1873–1921) were already established in their own studio when they met Mackintosh and his friend Herbert McNair at Glasgow School of Art. Margaret designed and painted the interiors of many of Mackintosh's most famous buildings, and advised and inspired him throughout his career. Her work was strange, stylised and otherworldly, inspired by ancient Celtic patterns, and often based on legends and fairy-tales. Because the images Margaret created were ethereal, even ghostly, the four friends were nicknamed 'the Spook School'.

The Glasgow Girls

The MacDonald sisters were just two of the accomplished female artists living and working in Scotland in the early twentieth century. Many trained at Glasgow School of Art (they were some of the first women allowed to study there) and / or belonged to the pioneering Glasgow Society for Women Artists, founded in 1882. Later historians have grouped them together as the 'Glasgow Girls'. Here are some of the most famous.

- Jessie Wylie Newbery (1864–1948): Embroiderer; won recognition for embroidery as a form of art; founded Department of Needlework at Glasgow School of Art.

- Bessie MacNicol (1869–1904): Painter noted for her use of colour, light and shade.

- Annie French (1872–1965): Illustrator and designer in sinuous Art Nouveau style.

- Ann Macbeth (1875–1948): Embroiderer; pioneer 'outreach' teacher of creative crafts. She believed that opportunities for art should be available to all, rich or poor, and encouraged women to design and make their own clothes, using inexpensive everyday materials. She often wore stylish garments she had made and embroidered herself.

- Jessie M King (1875–1949): Illustrator of children's books, potter and jeweller.

- Helen Paxton Brown (1876–1956): Embroiderer and painter. Inspired by the style and techniques of French Impressionist painters, her work was lively and vivid. She said she liked to 'play with colour'. Also created beautiful book-bindings and hand-painted ceramics.

- Christian Jane Fergusson (1876-1957): Landscape painter, admired for her images of the Scottish coast. Also created tapestries and metalwork, and was a keen teacher of art.

- De Courcy Lewthwaite Dewar (1878–1959): Silversmith; designer.

- Norah Neilson Gray (1882–1931): Portrait painter; first woman appointed to the hanging committee of prestigious Royal Glasgow Institute of the Fine Arts.

Old and New

The Glasgow Girls and other pioneering female professional artists are (quite rightly) celebrated today. However, they were not the first Scottish women to express themselves in visual media, or to earn a living from craft skills. For centuries, Scottish women from wealthy, leisured families sketched and painted. Some were very good. For example, the bird paintings of **Jemima Blackburn** (1823–1909) are remarkable for their detailed and original scientific observation, as well as for their beauty. And, before sewing and knitting machines were in widespread use (from the 1850s), countless poor females used craft skills passed on from woman to woman to earn a pittance making clothes and other household items.

Mrs Jameson and her flowerers

From around 1780, white embroidered muslin clothes were high fashion. In 1814, Mrs Marie Montgomerie, whose family came from Ayr, gave a beautiful robe, made in France, to her friend Mrs Jamieson, a cotton merchant's wife. Mrs Jamieson decided to copy its fine embroidery to decorate collars and indoor caps, and taught poor women living in Ayrshire how to stitch this intricate 'floo'ering' (flowering).

Mrs Jamieson's designs became very popular, and merchants in Glasgow sent out cloth ready-stamped with patterns for Scottish women and girls to sew at home, then return. The pay was poor and the work was exhausting. Whisky was recommended to bathe tired eyes, but the vision of many female 'flowerers' was ruined by the time they were thirty.

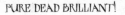
Not for women?

In spite of lack of opportunities to train or join the largely closed male worlds of art practitioners and consumers (art was 'by men, for men'), early Scottish women did manage to work and win respect as artists. One of the first we know of is **Esther Inglis** (1571–1624). The daughter of a (female) map-maker, she produced exquisite calligraphy and miniature portraits. Later women artists made careers as portrait painters, especially of women and children. Jacobite **Catherine Read** (1723–1778) fled to France after the 1745 rebellion, where she painted French and Scottish noble families; **Anne Forbes** (1745–1834) worked (respectably) as a drawing teacher in Edinburgh, but was also commissioned to paint portraits; adventurous **Christina Robertson** (1796–1854) was employed as a painter at the Russian imperial court.

Much more recently, Scotland's women artists have explored and celebrated how and what we see on (almost) equal terms with men. As Scottish-born painter **Dame Ethel Walker** (1861–1951) complained, after being complimented as 'a women artist' in 1938:

'There is no such thing as a woman artist. There are only two kinds of artist – bad and good. You can call me a good artist if you like.'

We cannot name them all. But we can't ignore Scotland's first modernist, abstract painter and printmaker, **Wilhelmina 'Willie' Barns-Graham** (1912–2004) whose dramatic works, inspired by landscape, have been called 'radiant' and 'free'. Or **Anne Redpath** (1895–1965) whose vibrant paintings experiment with pattern, colour and distorted perspective. Or **Dame Elizabeth Blackadder** (born 1931), the first woman member of both the Scottish Royal Academy and the Royal Academy in London – and also Her Majesty's Painter and Limner in Scotland. Her meditative still life paintings, often featuring flowers, reflect her interest in Japanese design. Perhaps best-known of all, **Joan Eardley** (1921–1963) painted emotional portraits of children from some of Glasgow's meanest streets, and also powerful images of the sea and sky of the Aberdeenshire coast. Adopted Scot **Gunnie Moberg** (1941–2007), originally from Sweden, recorded

Orkney people and landscapes in perceptive photographs. **Lotte Glob** (b 1944), from Denmark, creates ceramic art inspired by the wild beauty of Scotland's far north-west. And, while fine art it's not, Scottish illustrator **Mairi Hedderwick** (born 1939) has delighted children and recorded a unique way of life with witty and loving images of Hebridean crofters in her *Katie Morag* books.

Among younger Scottish women artists, **Alison Watt** (b 1965) has been praised for her extraordinarily detailed paintings of fabrics and textures, and **Susan Philipsz** (b 1965) won the 2010 Turner Prize for her sound installation sited on three Glasgow bridges. And, last but by no means least, **Muriel Gray** (b 1958), who trained as a designer, has made a unique and important contribution to Scottish cultural life, at first through her original, challenging work in television and more recently as first female chair of the board of governors of Glasgow School of Art.

❝ Oh wad some Power
the giftie gie us
To see ourselves as
others see us... ❞

Robert Burns, 1786

wad = would
giftie = gift
gie = give

POSTSCRIPT
– AS OTHERS
SEE US

ell, that's not a gift that all Scottish women in the past might have liked. Because the others who were looking at them were very often wrong. Scottish women were not inherently 'inferior' (page 195), and their achievements were not automatically 'weaker and poorer' (page 194). Nor were they always 'like a man's'. Women could, and did, dare to be different. By doing so, they helped shape Scotland, and, in many different ways, big or small, they changed the world.

For centuries, Scottish women's lives, interests and achievements were largely overlooked and forgotten. There are, for example, more statues of animals in Edinburgh than statues of women. Or maybe they were sidelined, or mythologised. Want a romantic heroine? Try Flora MacDonald! A warrior princess? What about Scáthach? A noble queen? St Margaret! A wicked queen? Lady Macbeth!! You'll find plenty of tough, defiant women workers in Glasgow. And if you're looking for picturesque peasants, there's no shortage in Scottish history: braw, handsome fishwives; bonny milkmaids wenching* in summer shielings* and coy, bare-legged Hieland lassies trampling the washing in mountain streams.*

* Wenching = courting (and more).
* Shielings = shelters in upland pastures, where young women (and some young men) took cows to graze in summer.
* A favourite subject for visiting male photographers in Victorian times (sigh).

Image...

Why were Scottish stereotypes so popular – and why are they still so widespread today? Because they were (and are) useful, even necessary. They are part of the Scottish everyday imagination, and also earn millions as cultural exports. Writing about classic Scottish films such as *Brigadoon* (1955) and *Local Hero* (1983), a female critic explains:

'...the physical experience of being in Scotland, and, of course, being connected with a woman who functions as the personification of Scotland, returns urban man to his contented, complete and natural self...'*

Men don't have all the fun, of course. For the past 200 years and more, romantic fictions of all kinds have dripped? bristled? – no, swaggered – with handsome Scottish heroes; there's one for every taste. 'Wild men, wild landscapes.'* Who could resist them?

* *Adrienne Scullion, in M Scriven and E Roberts (eds)* Group Identities on French and British Television, *2003, page 54.*
* The Scotsman, *11 February 2008.*

Looking further back in time, apart from the royal Scottish lion (which is male) and the Scottish Unicorn (who knows?), most characters symbolising Scotland and Scottish cities have been women, described by men. August Caledonia, chilly Scotia, elegant Edina (for Edinburgh) and grubby, motherly Glasgow. These women have not been individuals. Rather, as female Scottish writer and translator **Willa Muir** (1890–1970) described them, they were 'environments' for peoples and families.

Later writers also used women characters as symbols of Scotland. In Lewis Grassic Gibbon's novel, *Cloud Howe* (1933), the heroine's husband exclaims, on sensing her feelings of kinship with her homeland, 'Oh Chris Caledonia, I've married a nation!'

Very noble. However Gibbon also called the city of Aberdeen a 'thin-lipped peasant woman who has borne 11 and buried nine' and Dundee 'a frowsy fishwife addicted to gin and infanticide'.

Och, weel… Here's lookin' at you, too, Mr Gibbon.

...and Reality

Real-life Scottish women also make occasional appearances in the symbolic world, as inspiration for male creators. That was, and is, a tribute to their intellect, sympathetic character and beauty. But still through the eyes of men. Just a few examples...

'La Belle Stuart' beautiful Frances, Duchess of Richmond and Lennox (1647–1702): Model for the figure of Britannia that decorated UK coinage for centuries.

'The Artists's Wife' Margaret Lindsay of Evelick (c1726–1782): From a noble family, she eloped with her art teacher, brilliant but 'unrespectable' Scottish artist Allan Ramsay, and inspired some of his greatest works.

Clarinda: Agnes 'Nancy' Maclehose (1759–1841): The pretty, romantic, married poetry-lover to whom Robert Burns wrote one of his most famous love-lyrics 'Ae Fond Kiss' (1781).

'Highland Mary', **Margaret Mary Campbell** (1763–1786): Charming blue-eyed servant girl, immortalised in verses by Robert Burns. They were planning to elope together, but she died, pregnant, of typhoid fever. She is commemorated by a statue at Dunoon.

'The Belle of Mauchline': **Jean Armour** (1765–1834): Long-suffering wife of Robert Burns. While he was alive, her looks, character and singing all inspired him. After Burns's death, she became a devoted and respected guardian of his works and fame.

'Wha's like us?'

And so, in conclusion, what can we say? Generations of Scottish women and girls stretch back into the mists of time. Some we know about; most have been forgotten. But they are all part of Scotland's story.

As we have seen in this book, Scottish women were a very mixed bunch. They included females of towering intellect, tremendous practical achievement – often, to help others – patience, bravery, daring, dogged determination, wild imagination and wise (and foolish) political instincts. All they did took place under the gaze of men (plus women who shared male opinions). And that gaze was often indifferent, or hostile.

Can we name a real historical person to admire as the ideal Scottish woman? No; they were all so different. But when it comes to imaginary figures who symbolise past female lives in Scotland, we could go much further and do much worse than to choose beloved cartoon matriarch **Maw Broon**, created 1936, and still happily with us. (While considering cartoon characters, we might also remember gleeful, wild and sometimes wicked, schoolgirl Beryl the Peril, who first appeared in Dundee in 1953. As the daughter – and inspiration – of the artist who portrayed 'the Peril' remembered, 'Beryl was the start of young women asserting themselves, being as good as the boys…'.)

The great and the good, the rule-breakers and the law-changers, have their memorials. As indeed they should. But Maw Broon stands for Scottish history's ordinary, everyday, female norm. Although ample of figure, she represents the little people. She's good, and good fun: generous of heart, kindly, respectable, dependable, hard-working, devoted to her family and oh-so-capable. She shows us what almost everyone in Scotland's past (however hard they stared; whatever they wrote or said) believed Scottish women could be.

Like her or loathe her?

'Reductive tartan kitsch' *The Herald*, Glasgow 2009

'Two-dimensional black-and-white period piece' *The Sunday Times*, London 2009

'Robert Burns may be Scotland's greatest cultural icon, but the Broons aren't far behind with bairns of all ages around the world' *The Daily Telegraph*, London 2009

Reclaiming the Past

Scottish women's history may have languished in the shadows for far too long, but all is not lost. Today, Scotland has the only accredited museum dedicated to the study of women and their lives, past and present: Glasgow Women's Library. Opened in 1991 the Library is much, much more than a 'nationally significant' (Scottish Government) collection of books and a wonderful archive. It's a place for meeting, teaching and learning, a conference and training centre, a base for outreach work and home for projects of many different kinds. And it has a website with really useful information.

Brief timeline of Scottish history

c. 12,000–11,000 BC First modern humans visit Scotland.

c. 7000–5000 BC Humans settle in Scotland all year round.

c. 5000–4000 BC New settlers arrive from northwest Spain.

c. 4500–3000 BC First permanent villages and farms.

AD 79 Romans invade Scotland; build camps.

AD 84 Romans defeat Celtic tribes at Mons Graupius.

AD 122–128 Romans build Hadrian's Wall (northern England) as defence against Scots.

AD 139–163 Romans build Antonine Wall (central Scotland), then retreat.

AD 209 Earliest text naming Picts.

AD 342 Earliest text naming Scots (Irish Sea raiders).

AD 410 Romans abandon British Isles.

c. AD 500 First Christian missionaries reach Scotland.

AD 563 St Columba builds monastery on Iona.

AD 565 First text describing Loch Ness Monster.

AD 638 Angles conquer Edinburgh.

AD 685 Pictish king Bridei defeats Angles at Battle of Dunnichen.

AD 733 Bones of St Andrew arrive in Scotland.

AD 795–826 Vikings raid Iona.

AD 843 Kenneth MacAlpin crowned king of Picts and Scots.

AD 867–870 Vikings capture Strathclyde, Orkney and Shetland.

900 Constantine II names his kingdom Alba.

1004 Scottish slaves reach North America, with Vikings.

1040 Macbeth becomes king.

1066 Scots and English fight Vikings. Normans conquer England. Princess Margaret escapes to Scotland; marries Malcolm III.

1072 Normans invade Scotland; force Malcolm III to accept overlordship.

1098 Viking Magnus Barelegs conquers Hebrides.

1124 David I brings English and Normans to 'civilise' Scotland.

1174 Scots defeated by Henry II of England; forced to accept him as overlord.

1263 Alexander III defeats Vikings. Now rules most of Scotland except Orkney and Shetland.

1272 Edward I, 'Hammer of the Scots', becomes king of England.

1290 Death of Alexander's heir, the 'Maid of Norway'.

1292 John Balliol becomes King of Scots, with Edward I of England as overlord.

1295 Balliol joins with France against England: 'the Auld Alliance'.

1296 Edward I defeats Balliol; seizes Stone of Destiny.

1297 Wallace defeats Edward I at Stirling Bridge.

1305 Wallace executed. Robert the Bruce is king.

1314 Scots under Bruce defeat English at Bannockburn.

1320 Declaration of Arbroath (letter by Scots to Pope) demands Scotland's freedom.

1346 Stewart family grows powerful in Scotland.

1398 James IV conquers Lords of the Isles.

1560 Scots Parliament makes Scotland Protestant.

1561–1567 Mary Queen of Scots rules Scotland.

1567–1625 Reign of 'Wisest Fool' James VI.

1587 Mary Queen of Scots executed by English.

1603 Union of Crowns: James VI now James I of England.

1605 Gunpowder Plot in London targets James I.

1608 Scots Protestants settle in Northern Ireland.

1621 First Scots settle in Nova Scotia, Canada.

1638 Covenanters protest against King Charles I's religious policies.

1650 English Parliamentary army invades Scotland.

1681–1685 'Killing Time': Covenanters persecuted.

1688 'Glorious Revolution', James VII / II flees.

1689 'Bonnie Dundee' leads Jacobite rebellion.

1692 Massacre at Glencoe.

c. 1700–1800 Scots settle in North America and Caribbean.

1707 Act of Union: Scotland and England now United Kingdom.

1707–1800 Scots cities grow rich by trading in tobacco, sugar and slaves.

1715 Jacobite rebellion, led by James Edward Stuart, son of James VII / II.

1745–1746 Last Jacobite rebellion, led by Bonnie Prince Charlie.

1750s–1820 Growth of science and learning in Edinburgh. New Town built there.

c. 1750s–1850s Highland Clearances.

1759 Ironworks open at Carron; start of Industrial Revolution in Scotland.

c. 1780–1900 Scots industrial cities grow fast.

c. 1800–1950 Scots emigrate to Canada and Oceania.

1820 'Battle of Bonnybridge': Scottish workers demand political rights.

1846–1849 Scottish potato famine, plus cholera.

1860–1913 Scottish suffragette campaigns.

1880s Battles between crofters and landlords.

1914–1918 Many Scots soldiers die in World War I.

1919 'Red Clydesiders' call for better wages and working conditions.

1947 First Edinburgh Festival.

1950s–1970s Scottish new towns built.

1965–1969 North Sea oil and gas discovered.

1967 First Scottish Nationalist MP elected.

1996 Dolly the sheep cloned.

1997 Scots vote for devolution.

1999 Scottish Parliament meets again.

2000 Tourism now Scotland's biggest industry.

2007 Scottish National Party participates in Scotland's Government, for the first time ever.

2009 Singer Susan Boyle wins fame in TV talent show.

2013 Andy Murray is Wimbledon champion.

2014 Glasgow hosts Commonwealth Games.

2014 Year of Homecoming; Scotland welcomes overseas Scots.

2014 Scots vote to remain in the United Kingdom.

2015 Scottish National Party wins landslide victory.

2016 Welfare and tax powers devolved to Scottish Government.

2016 Scots vote to remain in European Union.

2017 New 'Queensferry Crossing' bridge.

2018 Glasgow School of Art on fire.

2018 European Championships held in Glasgow.

2018 Scotland's first Design Museum, at Dundee.

Index

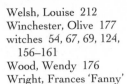

Cherished Library

Some other
Very Peculiar Histories®

The Blitz
David Arscott
ISBN: 978-1-907184-18-5

Castles
Jacqueline Morley
ISBN: 978-1-907184-48-2

Charles Dickens
Fiona Macdonald
ISBN: 978-1-908177-15-5

Golf
David Arscott
ISBN: 978-1-907184-75-8

Great Britons
Ian Graham
ISBN: 978-1-907184-59-8

Ireland
Jim Pipe
ISBN: 978-1-905638-98-7

Kings & Queens
Antony Mason
ISBN: 978-1-906714-77-2

London
Jim Pipe
ISBN: 978-1-907184-26-0

Scotland
Fiona Macdonald

Vol. 1: From ancient times
to Robert the Bruce
ISBN: 978-1-906370-91-6

Vol. 2: From the Stewarts
to modern Scotland
ISBN: 978-1-906714-79-6

Wales
Rupert Matthews
ISBN: 978-1-907184-19-2

Whisky
Fiona Macdonald
ISBN: 978-1-907184-76-5

For the full list, visit
www.salariya.com